PREFACE

1. Scope

This publication provides fundamental principles and guidance for the planning and conduct of joint military mobilization and demobilization, force expansion, use of volunteers, and Presidential Reserve Call-up.

2. Purpose

This publication has been prepared under the direction of the Chairman of the Joint Chiefs of Staff (CJCS). It sets forth joint doctrine to govern the activities and performance of the Armed Forces of the United States in operations and provides the doctrinal basis for interagency coordination and for US military involvement in multinational operations. It provides military guidance for the exercise of authority by combatant commanders and other joint force commanders (JFCs) and prescribes joint doctrine for operations and training. It provides military guidance for use by the Armed Forces in preparing their appropriate plans. It is not the intent of this publication to restrict the authority of the JFC from organizing the force and executing the mission in a manner the JFC deems most appropriate to ensure unity of effort in the accomplishment of the overall objective.

3. Application

a. Joint doctrine established in this publication applies to the commanders of combatant commands, subunified commands, joint task forces, subordinate components of these commands, the Services, and combat support agencies.

b. The guidance in this publication is authoritative; as such, this doctrine will be followed except when, in the judgment of the commander, exceptional circumstances dictate otherwise. If conflicts arise between the contents of this publication and the contents of Service publications, this publication will take precedence unless the CJCS, normally in coordination with the other members of the Joint Chiefs of Staff, has provided more current and specific guidance. Commanders of forces operating as part of a multinational (alliance or coalition) military command should follow multinational doctrine and procedures ratified by the United States. For doctrine and procedures not ratified by the United States, commanders should evaluate and follow the multinational command's doctrine and procedures, where applicable and consistent with US law, regulations, and doctrine.

For the Chairman of the Joint Chiefs of Staff:

DAVID L. GOLDFEIN, Lt Gen, USAF
Director, Joint Staff

Intentionally Blank

SUMMARY OF CHANGES
REVISION OF JOINT PUBLICATION 4-05
22 MARCH 2010

- Changes chapter titles to accurately reflect chapter content, i.e., mobilization or demobilization roles and responsibilities.

- Incorporates a discussion of the value of lessons learned throughout the mobilization process to enhance the planning of future mobilizations.

- Expands the discussion of global force management and how the tenets of assignment, allocation, and apportionment relate to mobilization planning.

- Provides discussion and definition of the Reserve Component (RC) as an operational force.

- Incorporates additional mobilization authorities including Title 10, United States Code (USC), 12304a and Title 10, USC, 12304b into the discussion of manpower mobilization options, levels of mobilization, and RC accessibility.

- Replaces occurrences of Joint Operation Planning and Execution System with the Adaptive Planning and Execution system.

- Updates the Joint Staff (JS) directorate mobilization responsibilities.

- Incorporates additional roles and responsibilities for a mobilization planner.

- Replaces all instances of the "United States Joint Forces Command" with the "JS J-3 [Operations Directorate] Joint Force Coordinator."

- Condenses the discussion of environmental impact on mobilization planning, eliminating extraneous information.

- Enhances the discussion of an individual augmentee to clarify and differentiate between a joint individual augmentee and individual Service augmentee.

- Updates the RC health services discussion to reflect that health service support is no longer a valid title, and that the joint medical analysis tool is no longer utilized.

- Incorporates a discussion of crisis action planning, comparing and contrasting with deliberate planning and explaining the relationship to mobilization.

- Clarifies combat commander responsibilities in the mobilization and demobilization process.

Intentionally Blank

TABLE OF CONTENTS

CHAPTER V
MOBILIZATION PLANNING AND EXECUTION

CHAPTER VI
JOINT DEMOBILIZATION PLANNING AND EXECUTION

APPENDIX

GLOSSARY

FIGURE

EXECUTIVE SUMMARY
COMMANDER'S OVERVIEW

- **Discusses Mobilization and National Security**

- **Provides the Mobilization Tenets**

- **Presents Mobilization Roles and Responsibilities**

- **Describes Twelve Representative Mobilization Actions in Resource Areas**

- **Covers Mobilization Planning and Execution**

- **Explains Joint Demobilization Planning and Execution**

Mobilization and National Security

Mobilization is the process of assembling and organizing national resources to support national objectives in time of war or other emergencies.

Mobilization includes assembling and organizing personnel and materiel for active duty military forces, activating the Reserve Component (RC) (including federalizing the National Guard), extending terms of service, surging and mobilizing the industrial base and training bases, and bringing the Armed Forces of the United States to a state of readiness for war or other national emergency. This description implies two processes:

- The **military mobilization process** by which the nation's Armed Forces are brought to an increased state of readiness.

- The **national mobilization process,** which mobilizes the interdependent resource areas to meet non-defense needs as well as sustaining the Armed Forces during all military operations.

The National Perspective

Congress has provided the President with a comprehensive menu of authorities for tailoring an appropriate response in a crisis. Several of these are available without a declaration of national emergency. Others require Presidential or congressional emergency declarations.

The Joint Military Perspective

Total joint force policy guides thorough mobilization planning and the development of procedures that are essential to the timely employment of reserve military power. The RC can augment capabilities primarily found in the Active Component (AC) or provide the sole or primary source of a capability not resident in the AC. In their operational roles, elements of the RC participate in a full range of missions according to their Services' force generation plans. The mobilization function includes activation (order to active duty [other than for training] in the federal service) of the RC, federalizing the National Guard, and surging and expanding the industrial base.

Mobilization Tenets

There are five mobilization tenets that describe the characteristics of successful mobilization and provide the foundation for mobilization doctrine.

The **five mobilization tenets** are:

- **Objective.** Joint operations are directed toward clearly defined, decisive, and achievable objectives. Planning for joint operations provides the basis for determining whether the mobilization of reserve forces and other resources are required to achieve the objectives.

- **Timeliness.** Timely mobilization of all resources is essential to achieving overwhelming force on the battlefield at the right time and place.

- **Unity of Effort.** Unity of effort in mobilization demands the integrated efforts of the nation's military and supporting resource areas toward achievement of common objectives.

- **Flexibility.** Flexibility for mobilization planning and execution has been provided for in Adaptive Planning and Execution and in the comprehensive set of legislated emergency powers that give the President, as Commander in Chief, wide latitude in crafting a response to a developing crisis.

- **Sustainability.** Mobilization sustainability is the ability to continuously provide logistics and personnel services necessary to maintain and prolong operations until successful mission completion. Timely, rapid mobilization planning is critical to ensuring logistics sustainability.

Mobilization Roles and Responsibilities

Joint Military Mobilization Planning and Execution

In times of crisis and war, the Office of the Secretary of Defense assists Secretary of Defense (SecDef) in managing the mobilization of the RC by developing implementation guidance for issue by SecDef or designated representative to the Joint Staff (JS), Military Departments, and Department of Defense (DOD) agencies. The DOD Master Mobilization Guide (MMG) contains basic guidance to direct and coordinate mobilization planning within DOD and implements DOD responsibilities under the National Security Council national security emergency preparedness policy.

Joint Planning and Execution Community

The **joint planning and execution community (JPEC)** collectively plans for the mobilization, deployment, employment, sustainment, redeployment, and demobilization of joint forces.

- The **JS J-4** [Logistics Directorate] is the focal point in the JS for integrating mobilization plans and coordinating mobilization execution.

- As part of their operation planning responsibilities, **combatant commanders (CCDRs)** identify and determine force and capability requirements, including time phased force deployment data as a part of developing campaign plans, contingency plans, and joint operation orders (OPORDs). The CCDRs are also responsible for identifying capability requirements of assigned RC forces and providing on-the-job training on theater-specific requirements when assigned forces are not on active duty or when they are on active duty for training.

- The **Military Departments and the United States Coast Guard** provide trained forces to the CCDRs. They prepare detailed mobilization plans identifying the actual forces and support to be provided and execute mobilization at the direction of SecDef.

Joint Deployment Process Owner and the Distribution Process Owner

The JS J-3 [Operations Directorate] Joint Force Coordinator as the joint deployment process owner serves as the DOD focal point to improve the joint deployment process. United States Transportation Command, as the distribution process owner, provides the strategic distribution capability to move forces and materiel in support of joint force commander operational requirements and to return personnel, equipment, and materiel to home and/or demobilization stations.

Mobilization Planner	The role of the mobilization planner is to assist DOD, Service, and joint forces in developing policies and procedures required to activate and inactivate RC personnel under peacetime and crisis response conditions. The mobilization planner provides subject matter expertise on the sourcing and employment of RC forces in support of the planning and execution of joint plans and orders.

Resource Areas

Twelve Representative Mobilization Actions in Resource Areas	Military mobilization requires the assembly and organization of resources in 12 interdependent resource areas (legal authorities, funding, environment, manpower, materiel and equipment, transportation, facilities, industrial base, training base, health services, communications, host-nation support).
Legal Authorities	There is a broad range of legal authority that enables or limits mobilization and emergency actions. Many of these authorities are available to the President in any level of emergency; others become available with a Presidential declaration of national emergency. Still others have been reserved by Congress pending passage of a public law or joint resolution of national emergency or declaration of war.
Funding	To facilitate mobilization for unplanned military operations, it is necessary to ensure that sufficient funding is available for known obligations.
Environment	Mobilization activities, particularly as they relate to facilities, may trigger the need for an environmental assessment or an environmental impact statement.
Manpower	Manpower mobilization augments the peacetime AC military end strength. Sources of military mobilization manpower include members of the RC, military retirees, volunteers with prior service, and nonprior service (NPS) personnel who volunteer. In addition to the call-up of manpower from reserve and retiree manpower pools, three other actions can be taken to ensure adequate manpower during mobilization. These are stop-loss, stop-movement, and personnel redistribution actions. Manpower mobilization options provide great flexibility to the President and SecDef for responding to a crisis.

Before a declaration of national emergency, the Secretaries of the Military Departments can call for RC volunteers who have needed skills and activate them for short periods of time.

When a governor requests **federal assistance in responding to a major disaster or emergency,** SecDef may order any member of the Army Reserve, Navy Reserve, Marine Corps Reserve, and Air Force Reserve to involuntary active duty up to 120 days per Title 10, United States Code (USC), Section 12304a.

A Presidential declaration of national emergency and invocation of the **partial mobilization** authority makes up to one million members of the Ready Reserve available for up to 24 consecutive months per Title 10, USC, Section 12302.

Full mobilization may be ordered in time of war or national emergency declared by Congress or when otherwise authorized by law per Title 10, USC, Section 12301(a).

Material and Equipment

The materiel and equipment resource area includes all classes of supply. It includes equipment on hand in units, remain-behind equipment in theater, war reserves, pre-positioned equipment, and the output of the depot maintenance system and industrial base. Additional sources include items in the security assistance pipelines and off-the-shelf items from domestic and foreign commercial sources.

Transportation

Transportation resources are required to support mobilization, deployment, employment, sustainment, redeployment, and demobilization operations. Mobilization activities are supported principally by intra-continental United States (CONUS) air, rail, highway, pipeline, port facilities, and inland waterway assets of commercial firms. Air Mobility Command assets can quickly be expanded by the Air National Guard, Air Force Reserves, and the airlift assets of the US Navy Reserve. Additionally, the fleet can be augmented via contract commercial charters, and through the Civil Reserve Air Fleet.

Facilities

Facilities with the capacity for supporting increased workloads during mobilization are obtained from the following sources: commercial facilities that support DOD in peacetime; unused and standby capacity at existing government facilities; and new capacity developed on property acquired by DOD through lease, purchase, or exercise of other legal means.

Industrial Base

The US industrial base includes commercial production facilities and government owned facilities. Industrial base expansion includes actions to accelerate production within the existing industrial infrastructure, add new production lines and factories, and implement provisions of the Defense Priorities and Allocation System.

Training Base

The Services expand their institutional training bases to train NPS personnel to support and sustain an expanded force structure. The training base also provides reclassification and refresher training for individual augmentees who need it.

Health Services

In time of national emergency, the transfer of members of the United States Public Health Service commissioned corps to DOD may also provide additional health service professionals. Theater health services and aeromedical support is expanded by calling up, transferring, and reassigning health and medical professionals, AC and RC health services units, and hospital ships deployed to the theater. The CONUS health services base is expanded, as necessary, to provide care for casualties returned from the theater.

Communications

Although the US military utilizes its own communications systems to execute many national defense/crisis response requirements, it frequently relies upon commercial providers to fulfill its administrative support needs.

Host-Nation Support

Manpower, equipment, facilities, and services provided by host or allied nations during war or emergency can offset requirements for corresponding US military resources that are not affordable or practical to maintain in peacetime.

Mobilization Planning and Execution

Mobilization plans explain how force and resource expansion is to be accomplished.

Mobilization plans are detailed plans prepared by the Military Departments and DOD agencies. They are based on policy and planning guidance in the Guidance for Employment of the Force, Defense Planning Guidance,

Global Force Management Implementation Guidance, DOD MMG, and in tasks specified by the Chairman of the Joint Chiefs of Staff (CJCS) in the Joint Strategic Capabilities Plan.

Mobilization Planning

Chairman of the Joint Chiefs of Staff Instruction 3110.13, *Mobilization Guidance for the Joint Strategic Capabilities Plan (U)*, guides the Military Departments and CCDRs in preparing mobilization plans that support the CCDRs' contingency plans. During the joint operation planning process (JOPP), the Military Departments furnish mobilization-related information to the CCDRs, who incorporate it into the operation plan (OPLANs) under development or revision.

Mobilization Estimate of the Situation

The mobilization estimate provides a tool for mobilization planners to make a systematic appraisal of mobilization requirements and options. The mobilization estimate requires input from all functional areas of the JS, Service staffs, and the corresponding staff sections at the combatant commands.

Mobilization Planning During Deliberate Planning

During peacetime, mobilization planners in the JPEC participate in two primary activities: maintaining a mobilization base and participating in JOPP to develop detailed mobilization plans to support OPLANs.

Mobilization Execution

CJCS recommends to SecDef the assets that are to be called up and their planned use when RC forces are to be mobilized to augment the AC. SecDef approval is required for the execution of a mobilization OPORD. After the President's decision to initiate mobilization, SecDef directs the Military Departments to proceed. The Services publish mobilization orders in accordance with their respective procedures.

Monitoring the Status and Progress of Mobilization

Information received by proponents in each of the resource areas is analyzed and coordinated with the other resource area proponents to provide decision makers with recommendations for controlling, replanning, redirecting, or stopping mobilization operations.

Mobilization Reporting

The mobilization planner responds to formal and informal reporting requirements. Three formal reports are generated: RC requirements from annex A (Task Organization) of each OPLAN which lists the total RC requirements; the mobilization report; and during partial mobilization, the President's report to Congress.

Joint Demobilization Planning and Execution

Introduction

Demobilization is the process of transitioning from a conflict situation or from a wartime military establishment and defense-based civilian economy to a peacetime configuration while maintaining national security and economic vitality.

Demobilization and National Security

From a national perspective, the results of a successful demobilization process should put the US in a position to respond to future challenges to our national security.

Demobilization Planning

Demobilizing the Armed Forces could be a relatively straightforward return of mobilized/activated units and individuals to their former status. It could also be a broader process including measures such as deactivation of units, rapid discharge of individuals, and a major reorganization of the RC.

Recovery Planning

Recovery planning should be closely coordinated with demobilization planning. Recovery includes the reset actions necessary in the theater and CONUS base to restore force readiness and a credible capability to respond, in the short term, to a future threat.

Demobilization Execution

Following redeployment, the Military Departments deactivate units or return them to a reserve status. Military personnel are released from active duty or returned to reserve status. Materiel and equipment may be returned to bases of origin or other reserve/guard units, moth-balled, stored, distributed to other nations through foreign military sales or other security assistance programs, destroyed, sold for scrap, or turned over to the Defense Logistics Agency Disposition Services.

CONCLUSION

This publication provides fundamental principles and guidance for the planning and conduct of joint military mobilization and demobilization, force expansion, use of volunteers, and Presidential Reserve Call-up.

CHAPTER I
MOBILIZATION AND NATIONAL SECURITY

"The Congress shall have power . . . To provide for calling forth the Militia to execute the Laws of the Union, suppress Insurrections and repel Invasions; To provide for organizing, arming, and disciplining the Militia, and for governing such part of them as may be employed in the Service of the United States, reserving to the States respectively, the Appointment of the officers, and the Authority of training the Militia according to the discipline prescribed by Congress."

Constitution of the United States of America, Article I, Section 8

1. Introduction

a. **Mobilization is the process of assembling and organizing national resources to support national objectives in time of war or other emergencies.** Mobilization includes assembling and organizing personnel and materiel for active duty military forces, activating the Reserve Component (RC) (including federalizing the National Guard), extending terms of service, surging and mobilizing the industrial base and training bases, and bringing the Armed Forces of the United States to a state of readiness for war or other national emergency. This description implies two processes:

(1) The **military mobilization process** by which the nation's Armed Forces are brought to an increased state of readiness.

(2) The **national mobilization process,** which mobilizes the interdependent resource areas (see Chapter IV, "Resource Areas") to meet non-defense needs as well as sustaining the Armed Forces during all military operations.

b. A **responsive mobilization capability** is critical to our national security and the execution of the President's national security strategy (NSS) and its derivatives, the national defense strategy (NDS), and the national military strategy (NMS). The US employs its military capabilities at home and abroad in support of its strategies in a variety of operations. This chapter examines the relationship between mobilization and national security. It concludes with a discussion of demobilization, an essential first step toward maintaining national security after a crisis or war.

2. The National Perspective

a. The **NSS.** The NSS provides a broad strategic context for employing military capabilities in concert with other instruments of national power. In the ends, ways, and means construct, the NSS provides the ends.

b. The **NDS.** The NDS, signed by the Secretary of Defense (SecDef), outlines the Department of Defense's (DOD's) approach to implementing the President's NSS. The NDS supports the NSS by establishing a set of overarching defense objectives that guides DOD's security activities and provides direction for the NMS. The NDS objectives serve as links between military activities and those of other United States Government (USG) departments and agencies in pursuit of national goals. This document provides the ways in the ends, ways, and means construct.

c. The **NMS**

(1) **The NMS,** signed by the Chairman of the Joint Chiefs of Staff (CJCS), supports the aims of the NSS and implements the NDS. It describes the Armed Forces' plan to achieve military objectives in the near term and provides a vision for maintaining a force capable of meeting future challenges. It also provides focus for military activities by defining a set of interrelated military objectives and joint operating concepts from which the combatant commanders (CCDRs) and Service Chiefs identify desired capabilities and against which the CJCS assesses risk. This provides the final piece of the ends, ways, and means construct—the means. **Explicit in the military strategy is the assertion that we can meet the challenges of the foreseeable future with a total joint force**—a carefully tailored combination of Active Component (AC) and RC (including Retired Reserve), together with retired military personnel, DOD civilian employees, and DOD contractors. **Implicit in the military strategy is the need to maintain and improve the capability to rapidly and efficiently mobilize forces and resources** to respond to natural disaster challenges at the low end of the range of military operations and to deter or counter a broad spectrum of serious threats to our national security, such as threats to the homeland.

(2) Figure I-1 depicts a representative range of military commitments together with the levels of mobilization and emergency authorities available to the President when RC forces are needed for an appropriate response. **Congress has provided the President with a comprehensive menu of authorities for tailoring an appropriate response in a crisis.** Several of these are available without a declaration of national emergency. Others require Presidential or congressional emergency declarations.

d. **Global Force Management (GFM).** **The GFM process integrates force assignment, apportionment, and allocation.** It provides comprehensive insights into the global availability of US military forces and capabilities, and provides senior decision makers a process to quickly and accurately assess the impact and risk of proposed changes in assigning, apportioning, and allocating forces and capabilities among combatant commands (CCMDs). Two important attributes of GFM include being able to globally assess force sourcing risk in order to address mitigation options and enabling global sourcing with the best force sourcing option, regardless of command, organization, or Service to which the force or personnel are assigned. The SecDef's Global Force Management Implementation Guidance (GFMIG) integrates complementary assignment, allocation, and apportionment information into a single authoritative document in support of DOD's strategic guidance. See the GFMIG for additional detail.

e. **Force Sourcing—Assignment, Allocation, and Apportionment**

(1) Title 10, United States Code (USC), delineates responsibilities for assignment, allocation, and apportionment of forces. SecDef assigns forces/capabilities, allocates

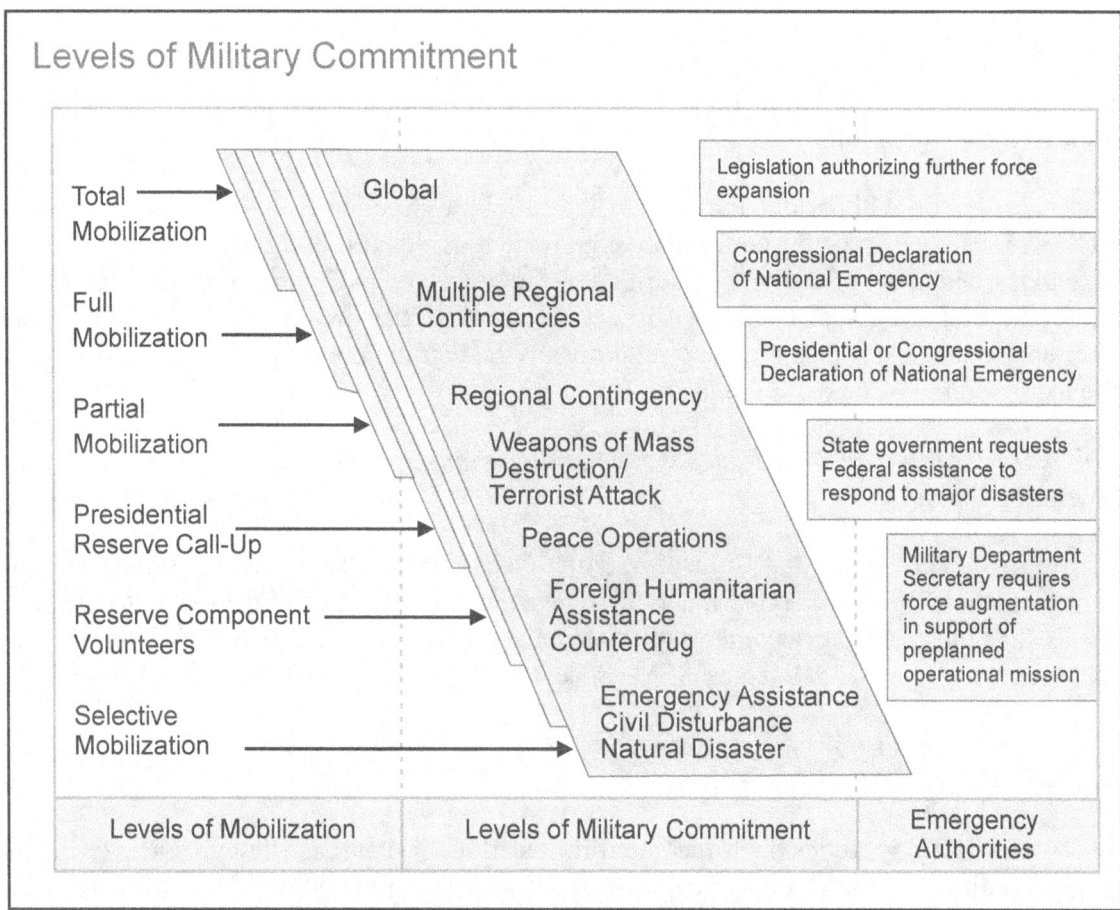

Figure I-1. Levels of Military Commitment

forces/capabilities, provides planning guidance to CCMDs, and provides overarching strategic guidance to the CJCS.

(2) **GFM supports decision making by integrating the three processes of assignment, apportionment, and allocation.** This integration aligns operational forces with known apportionment and allocation requirements in advance of planning and deployment preparation timelines.

(a) **Assignment.** Title 10, USC, Sections 161, 162, and 167 outline force assignment guidance and requirements. The President, through the Unified Command Plan (UCP), instructs SecDef to document his direction for assigning forces in the *Forces for Unified Commands Memorandum (Forces For)*. The Secretaries of the Military Departments shall assign forces under their jurisdiction to unified and specified CCMDs to perform missions assigned to those commands. Such assignment defines the combatant command (command authority) and shall be made as directed by SecDef, including the command to which forces are to be assigned. Assignment is further explained in the biennial GFMIG.

(b) **Apportionment.** Apportionment is the distribution of forces and capabilities as a starting point for planning. Pursuant to Title 10, USC, Section 153, "The

CJCS shall be responsible for preparing strategic plans, including plans which conform with resource levels projected by SecDef to be available for the period of time for which the plans are to be effective." Forces apportioned for planning purposes may not be those allocated for execution.

(c) **Allocation.** Pursuant to Title 10, USC, Section 162, "[a] force assigned to a CCMD… may be transferred from the command to which it is assigned only by authority of SecDef; and under procedures prescribed by the Secretary and approved by the President." Under this authority, SecDef allocates forces between CCDRs. When transferring forces, the Secretary will specify the command relationship the gaining commander will exercise and the losing commander will relinquish.

For more information on GFM, see the GFMIG, and Joint Publication (JP) 5-0, Joint Operation Planning.

(3) The UCP, the Joint Strategic Capabilities Plan (JSCP), Guidance for Employment of the Force (GEF), and JP 1, *Doctrine for the Armed Forces of the United States,* are the baseline documents that establish the policy framework and inform the GFMIG, which further delineates GFM processes:

(a) Provides direction from SecDef regarding assignment of forces to CCDRs;

(b) Includes the force/capabilities allocation process that provides CCMDs access to all available military or DOD resources for both rotational requirements and requests for capabilities or forces in response to crises or emergent contingencies;

(c) Includes apportionment guidance provided in the JSCP; and

(d) Informs joint force, structure, and capability assessment processes.

(4) GFM informs DOD's assessment processes by identifying sporadic or persistent under-sourced or hard-to-source forces/capabilities.

(5) The Joint Staff (JS) J-3 [Operations Directorate] Joint Force Coordinator focuses on the global allocation of capabilities and forces to support CCMD requirements. The JS J-3 Joint Force Coordinator uses GFM Board-developed and approved guidance to recommend global sourcing solutions. CCMDs, Military Departments, and the National Guard Bureau provide force/capability commitment, availability, and readiness data to the JS J-3 Joint Force Coordinator. Additionally, the JS J-3 Joint Force Coordinator assesses the ability to sustain joint presence, operational commitments, and global surge capabilities over time based on allocation decision/actions in effect. Reporting on the readiness, disposition, and development of sourcing recommendations for forces/capabilities sourced by United States Special Operations Command (USSOCOM), United States Strategic Command, and United States Transportation Command (USTRANSCOM) will be coordinated by those CCMDs with the Services and other CCDRs to CJCS.

3. The Joint Military Perspective

a. **Total Joint Force Policy.** The total joint force policy is one **fundamental premise upon which our military force structure is built.** Mobilization activities require the support of the private sector (employers and community), DOD civilian workforce, and contractor support. Total joint force policy guides thorough **mobilization planning** and the **development of procedures that are essential to the timely employment of reserve military power.** SecDef issued a directive on managing the RC as an operational force to further codify total joint force policy.

b. **RC as an Operational Force.** The RC provides operational capabilities and strategic depth to meet US defense requirements across the full spectrum of conflict. The RC can augment capabilities primarily found in the AC or provide the sole or primary source of a capability not resident in the AC. In their operational roles, elements of the RC participate in a full range of missions according to their Services' force generation plans. Units and individuals participate in missions in an established cyclic or periodic manner that provides predictability for the CCMDs, the Services, Service members, their families, and employers. Preplanned mobilization support, per Title 10, USC, Section 12304b, gives the Secretaries of the Military Departments the authority to activate their selected Reserves up to 365 days to augment the active forces for preplanned missions in support of a CCMD, thus utilizing the RC as an operational force with cyclical predictability. In their strategic roles, RC units and individuals train or are available for missions in accordance with the NDS. As such, the RC provides strategic depth and is available to transition to operational roles as needed.

c. **Mobilization and Demobilization in Joint Planning and Operations.** The **Adaptive Planning and Execution (APEX)** system is the principal system within DOD for translating policy decisions into operation plans (OPLANs) and operation orders (OPORDs) in support of national security objectives. The joint operation planning process (JOPP) is an integral part of APEX, serving as an adaptive and collaborative tool in supporting deliberate planning and crisis action planning (CAP).

TOTAL JOINT FORCE POLICY

The total joint force policy was used during Operations DESERT SHIELD and DESERT STORM and more recently, Operations ENDURING FREEDOM and IRAQI FREEDOM, which involved the largest mobilization and deployment of reserve forces since the Korean War. The US military relied on military retirees, Department of Defense civilian personnel, and contractor personnel for critical skills and performance of many essential tasks.

Various Sources

---

(1) Mobilization

(a) **The mobilization function includes activation** (order to active duty [other than for training] in the federal service) **of the RC, federalizing the National Guard, and surging and expanding the industrial base.** Figure I-2 illustrates levels of mobilization.

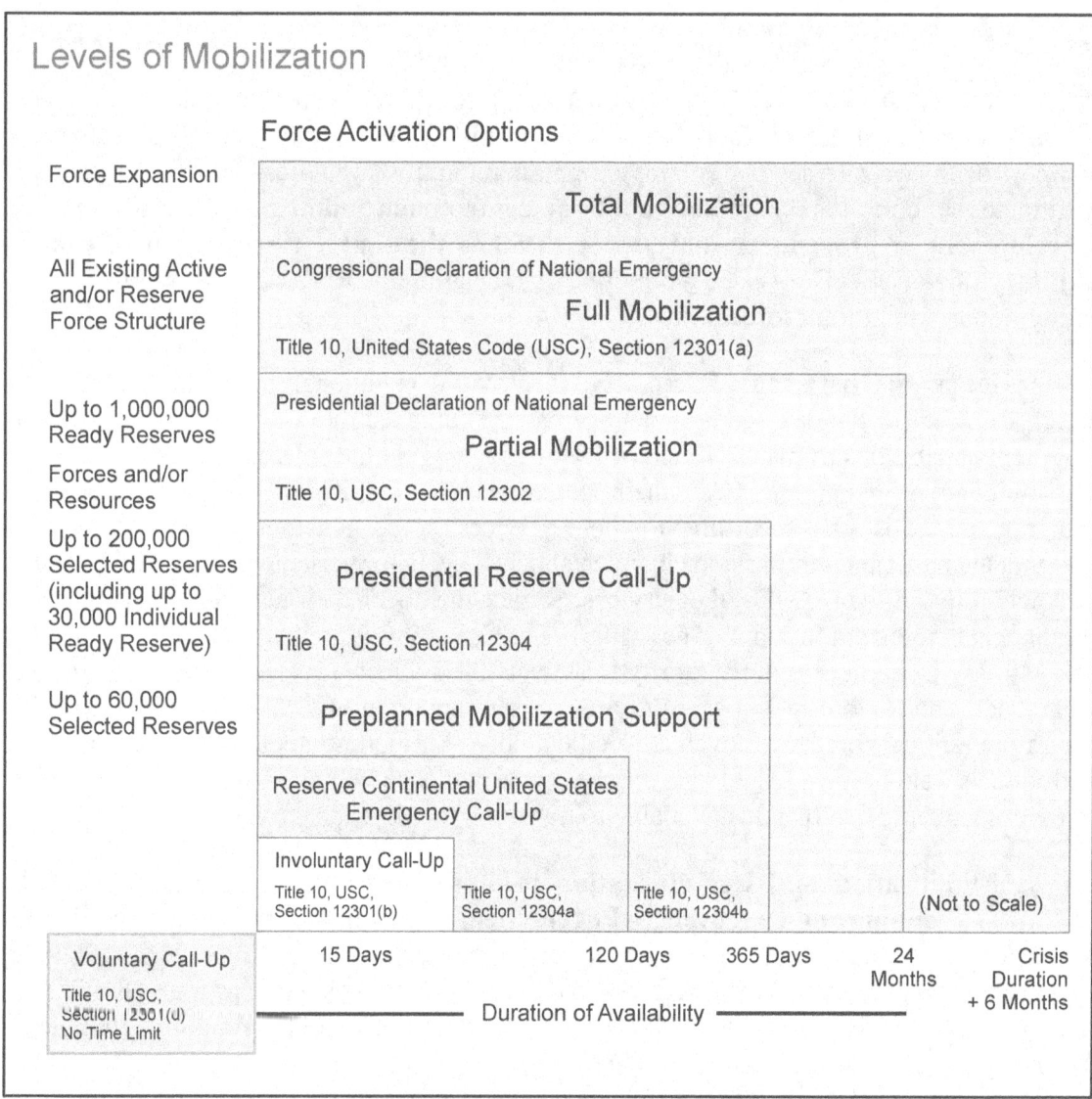

Figure I-2. Levels of Mobilization

(b) Because the most visible mobilization activity is the activation of RC members, military planners tend to focus planning on manpower issues. **Mobilization**, however, **involves much more than expanding and filling the military force with people.** The force must be equipped, trained, and sustained over time if it is to achieve and maintain its designed capability. Mobilization activities require the **support of the private sector (employers and community), DOD civilian workforce, contractors, and Service members' families.** Mobilized activities also require **increased resources** in the areas of materiel, transportation, facilities, industrial production, training base capacity, health services, and communications. Actions may be required to ensure continued compliance with, or obtain temporary waivers of environmental protection laws. The US military requires adequate funding and sufficient legal authorities to initiate and sustain mobilization activities. **Mobilization**, therefore, **includes determining and satisfying demands for those resources required to support the total joint force** during deployment, employment, sustainment, and redeployment. RC call-up decision making involves a formal process that recognizes the balance between the JS, the RC leadership, and the Office of the Secretary of Defense (OSD). Figure I-3 illustrates responsibilities associated with RC call-up decision making.

RESERVE COMPONENT CALL-UP DECISION MAKING							
Mobilization Planning Community	Pre-Mobilization Review and Coordination	Educate Senior Leadership on RC Potential	Review Policies for Use of RC	Confirm Preplanned Mobilization Capabilities	Recommend Changes in Peacetime Budgeting Priorities	Mobility Demobilization Policy to Suit Contingency	Prepare Decision Packages
Common Activities (For all)	Identify point of contact network Convene preliminary meetings focused on "what if" questions using current information Analyze lessons learned from similar crises Consider potential supporting requirements Manage media relations and coordinate with public affairs officer	Conduct meetings and/or briefings on RC mobilization policies: availability, mobilization and deployment criteria, call-up procedures, and the different categories of RC and their potential use	Review and modify call-up instructions and procedures Recommend modifications and exceptions to policy Coordinate with legal counsel Review policies and/or procedures for "conscientious objectors" and Service members Civil Relief Act	Estimate ability of mobilization activities to meet plan schedule Identify capability shortfalls	Review unfunded mobilization requirements Coordinate with resource area proponents for adjustments to internal funding priorities	Initiate planning for the return of RC to civilian status	Respond to information requests as appropriate
Joint Staff	Become familiar with RC call-up procedures Review operation plan Be prepared to recommend level of call-up	Review legal authorities Review mobilization plans, policies, and procedures Brief leadership on call-up authorities and specific qualities of RC	Identify opportunities for joint use of Service mobilization assets Monitor development of RC deployment criteria	Confirm monitoring and reporting systems: coordinate reporting requirements	Seek opportunities for cross-Service utilization of RC assets	Seek opportunities for cross-Service utilization of RC demobilization facilities and assets	Prepare Draft Decision Package Staff Draft Decision Package with Services Forward Package to Chairman of Joint Chiefs of Staff
Legend RC Reserve Component							

Figure I-3. Reserve Component Call-Up Decision Making

(c) **Mobilization planning complements and supports joint operation planning.** It is accomplished primarily by the Services and their major subordinate commands based on SecDef guidance. It requires development of supporting plans by other USG departments and agencies. Just as the Services mobilize their reserve organizations and individuals to augment military capability, **supporting USG departments and agencies must oversee mobilization of the support base required to sustain the mobilized force.**

Detailed discussions of mobilization levels and emergency authorities are provided in Chapter IV, "Resource Areas," and Chapter V, "Mobilization Planning and Execution."

(d) The JS supports the CJCS's role as principal military advisor to the President and SecDef; facilitates resolution of conflicts for scarce resources among the Services, CCDRs, and DOD agencies; provides input for resolution of claims for resources between the military and civil sectors in wartime; and oversees mobilization planning. To facilitate the CJCS's role in such mobilization matters, the mobilization working group (MWG) has been established. The MWG is chaired by the JS J-4 [Logistics Directorate] Strategy and Readiness Division, assisted by the Force Mobilization Branch Chief. The MWG is designed to enhance communications among OSD, the JS, and the Services when military operations warrant the use of the RC.

Appendix D, "Mobilization Working Group," contains specific policy and procedures related to the MWG.

(2) **Demobilization.** Demobilization is **the process of transitioning from a conflict or wartime military establishment and defense-based civilian economy to a peacetime configuration while maintaining national security and economic vitality.** Implied in this description are two types of activities: those associated with reducing the percentage of the nation's production capacity devoted to the Armed Forces and defense industry, and those undertaken to maintain national security and economic vitality. These tasks, which historically compete for resources, can make the management of demobilization even more complex and challenging than mobilization.

Demobilization planning and execution are covered in Chapter VI, "Joint Demobilization Planning and Execution."

**MANAGING THE RESERVE COMPONENT
AS AN OPERATIONAL FORCE**

It is the Department of Defense policy that:

a. The Reserve Component (RC) provides operational capabilities and strategic depth to meet US defense requirements across the full spectrum of conflict including under Title 10, United States Code (USC), Sections 12301, 12302, 12304, and 12306.

b. The Active Component and RC are integrated as a total force based on the attributes of each component and its core competencies.

---

c. Homeland defense and defense support of civil authorities are total force missions. Unity of effort is maintained consistent with statutory responsibilities in operations involving federal forces and non-federalized National Guard forces with federal forces under federal command and control and non-federalized National Guard forces under state command and control.

d. The RC provides connection to and commitment of the American public.

e. The continuum of service is utilized to enhance the effectiveness of and sustain the all-volunteer force with flexible service options that are attractive to a broad population.

f. Utilization rules are implemented to govern frequency and duration of activations. Since expectation management is critical to the success of the management of the RC as an operational force, these rules enhance predictability and judicious and prudent use of the RC.

g. Voluntary duty, per Title 10, USC, Section 12301d and Title 32, USC, Section 502(f)(2) is encouraged to meet mission requirements.

h. The RC is resourced to meet readiness requirements per Title 10, USC, Sections 3013, 5013, and 8013. RC resourcing plans shall ensure visibility to track resources from formulation, appropriation, and allocation through execution.

i. Outreach services are established and available for RC members, their families, and employers from pre-activation through reintegration.

Robert M. Gates, Secretary of Defense
29 October 2008

Intentionally Blank

CHAPTER II
MOBILIZATION TENETS

"The AC [Active Component] and RC [Reserve Component] are fully integrated partners in executing US military strategy, to include HD [homeland defense] and defense support of civil authorities (DSCA) operations."

Joint Publication 1,
Doctrine for the Armed Forces of the United States

1. Introduction

There are five mobilization tenets that describe the characteristics of successful mobilization and **provide the foundation for mobilization doctrine.** The tenets are: **objective, timeliness, unity of effort, flexibility, and sustainability.**

2. Mobilization Tenets

a. **Objective. Joint operations are directed toward clearly defined, decisive, and achievable objectives.** Planning for joint operations provides the basis for determining whether the mobilization of reserve forces and other resources are required to achieve the objectives. **Commanders and operational planners must clearly understand the mobilization implications associated with their plans** to ensure that needed resources are identified, mobilized, protected, and used effectively. Requirements for activating RC forces must be clearly identified, as well as the need to expand the capability or capacity of other resource areas. **Commanders and operational and mobilization planners must coordinate their efforts** to ensure they clearly understand the time required for mobilization actions, they identify the limitations associated with industrial and civil mobilization, and they address the resulting impacts.

b. **Timeliness.** Timely mobilization of all resources is essential to achieving overwhelming force on the battlefield at the right time and place. It is also essential to seizing and maintaining the initiative. We must be able to act faster than the adversary is able to react. **Achieving effective mobilization of resources requires timely indications and warnings** of the threat and appropriate response to such indications and warnings; **efficient mobilization procedures** and frequent exercises and rehearsals; **RC** forces with the resources necessary to maintain required readiness levels; a supportive employer and community base; a **civilian workforce** prepared to support military missions; **contractors** prepared for their roles; **stockpiles** of materiel and equipment to sustain the force until industrial base output can be expanded; and **synchronized plans** for the expansion of transportation, facilities, training base, health services, communications, and other support necessary to deploy, employ, sustain, redeploy, and, when appropriate, demobilize forces.

TIMELINESS FROM 20TH CENTURY WARS

Timeliness has always been a major problem in mobilization. In World War I, industrial mobilization was geared to a projected big push planned for the summer of 1919. The surprising success of the last-ditch German offensive in the spring of 1918, followed that autumn by the climactic Allied counteroffensive, precipitated the commitment of US troops to combat armed and equipped with British and French rather than American supplies and weaponry.

In World War II, personnel mobilization could never be completely synchronized with requirements. The result was a recurrent boom and bust cycle with regard to enlisted and junior officer replacements. Partially trained troops repeatedly had to be stripped out of units in training to fill up units in combat or about to be deployed, thereby delaying the combat readiness of later deploying units.

The rapid demobilization after World War II, and neglect of military readiness in the immediate postwar period, left the United States without a viable capability for responding to a crisis that arose with little or no warning. The unfortunate result was that we were woefully unprepared for the surprise North Korean attack on South Korea in June 1950. We conducted a desperate delaying action, and were nearly forced off the Korean peninsula at Pusan, before reinforcing units and other resources could be mobilized and deployed to effectively counter the initial North Korean offensive.

Major mobilization decisions during Operation DESERT SHIELD/DESERT STORM were deliberately synchronized with United Nations resolutions and US congressional action. In so doing, these decisions not only satisfied the operational requirements of our joint military forces, they also provided clear signals of US resolve to adversaries, allies, and the US public, whose continuing policy support was critical to its success.

Various Sources

c. **Unity of Effort. Unity of effort in mobilization demands the integrated efforts of the nation's military and supporting resource areas** toward achievement of common objectives. **Integration is achieved through the effective use of planning and execution processes** that provide for timely and thorough coordination within the chain of command and among DOD, other USG departments and agencies, and the private sector. A manpower call-up, without employer and community support, is not sustainable over a long period of time. The failure to integrate mobilization activities within and among the various resource areas could delay the arrival of units and individual replacements in the operational area or impair their combat effectiveness.

UNITY OF EFFORT: WORLD WAR I

The absence of unity of effort contributed to a confusing and wasteful World War I mobilization. Only the most rudimentary advance planning had been accomplished before the US declaration of war in April 1917.

There was little coordination of personnel and materiel acquisition activities. Hundreds of thousands of conscripts reported to hastily constructed training installations that would not be supplied with enough organizational clothing, equipment, and weapons to properly equip them for several months.

The Government, civilian economy, and Services competed for resources without a competent coordinating authority. War production was chaotic. Priorities for raw materials, labor, and electric power were determined in ad hoc negotiations among public and private officials. East Coast ports of embarkation were quickly overwhelmed, and inland transportation became so congested that the President was forced to nationalize the country's railroad system.

A sealift shortage, evident even before German submarines began sinking merchant ships faster than new ones could be built, cast doubts on the nation's ability to deploy forces to Europe even after they were trained and equipped. The net result was that half-trained US forces were sent to France in British vessels. The forces were largely equipped with British and French artillery, tanks, machine guns, and aircraft, and were required to undergo further training before they could be used effectively on the battlefield.

Various Sources

d. **Flexibility.** Flexibility is necessary to develop an appropriate response in a crisis, overcome unforeseen problems, adapt to uncertainties, and adjust to the friction of war. **Flexibility for mobilization planning and execution has been provided for in APEX** and in the comprehensive set of legislated emergency powers that give the President, as Commander in Chief, wide latitude in crafting a response to a developing crisis. **Substantial emergency authorities are available to the President before a declaration of national emergency,** such as the Presidential Reserve Call-up (PRC) authority and authorities establishing the priority of industrial production for defense needs. Other authorities are made available to the President upon a declaration of national emergency. The National Emergencies Act states that when the President declares a national emergency, he must specify the powers he is invoking. Although the powers are limited to those specifically invoked, others may be subsequently invoked. This provides **the President the flexibility to act incrementally to signal US resolve in developing crises** and to authorize certain preparatory actions without causing undue provocation. **APEX also provides flexibility in mobilization** by delegating authority to the maximum extent consistent with control to promote freedom of action by subordinates and ensure continuity when communications are disrupted. **The joint planning and execution community (JPEC) also contributes to flexibility** by developing a wide range of military response options for consideration by decision makers. **Flexibility also demands a system to accurately monitor the status and**

progress of mobilization and the ability to replan, reprogram, and redirect mobilization activities to work around bottlenecks and resource shortfalls, and for providing protection of the force, equipment, and infrastructure being mobilized.

FLEXIBILITY: OPERATION DESERT SHIELD/DESERT STORM

Flexibility overcame limitations in planning, force structure, and capabilities in a number of instances during Operation DESERT SHIELD/DESERT STORM in 1990-1991. The availability of pre-positioned supplies and a fairly extensive host-nation infrastructure enabled the combatant commander to turn the absence of a fully developed deployment and transportation schedule to tactical advantage at the beginning of the crisis by gambling on the deployment of combat elements at the expense of logistic and administrative support units.

Forces deployed to the theater had insufficient organic transportation capability to carry out the campaign plan. Intensive efforts by the Joint Staff and the Department of State mobilized critical ground transport from host-nation and allied assets to execute the planned offensive.

The decision to deploy the US Army's VII Corps from Europe showed considerable flexibility. Besides powerful combat forces, VII Corps also included a fully structured support command, which proved extremely useful in addressing theater logistic shortfalls.

Although Operation DESERT SHIELD/DESERT STORM did not provide a truly strenuous test of production surge capabilities, industry did accelerate output of critical supplies, equipment, and munitions. Perhaps the best example of flexibility in this area was the deployment of a system prototype still undergoing developmental testing, the Joint Surveillance Target Attack Radar System aircraft. Its advanced technology gave the combatant commander the capability to monitor the battlefield and look deep behind enemy lines in a way never before possible.

Various Sources

---

e. **Sustainability.** Mobilization sustainability is the ability to continuously provide logistics and personnel services necessary to maintain and prolong operations until successful mission completion. Timely, rapid mobilization planning is critical to ensuring logistics sustainability. **Sustainability in joint operations provides the joint force commander (JFC) flexibility, endurance, and the ability to extend operational reach.** To maintain sustainability, commanders must ensure personnel services, health services, field services, quality of life, and general supply support are adequate. Effective sustainment determines the depth to which the joint force can conduct decisive operations, allowing the JFC to seize, retain, and exploit the initiative. Sustainment is primarily the responsibility of the supported CCDR and subordinate Service component commanders in close cooperation with the Services, combat support agencies (CSAs), and supporting commands.

CHAPTER III
MOBILIZATION ROLES AND RESPONSIBILITIES

> *"Force projection allows a JFC [joint force commander] to position and concentrate forces to set the conditions for mission success."*
>
> **Joint Publication 3-35,**
> ***Deployment and Redeployment Operations***

1. Introduction

This chapter describes roles and responsibilities for joint military mobilization planning and execution. These roles and responsibilities extend from the President and SecDef down through the CCMDs, Services, and DOD agencies to installations for the entire process to be complete. The roles and responsibilities of the various USG departments and agencies that mobilize national resources to support and sustain the nation's military forces in time of war are outside the scope of this publication, but it is important to understand that virtually every USG department and agency would provide significant support to DOD if warranted by an emergency situation.

2. Joint Military Mobilization Planning and Execution

a. **OSD**

(1) **In times of crisis and war, OSD assists SecDef in managing the mobilization of the RC** by developing implementation guidance for issue by SecDef or designated representative to the JS, Military Departments, and DOD agencies. OSD assembles cost data and compiles reports on the cost of military operations, as required by law.

(2) **The DOD Master Mobilization Guide (MMG) contains basic guidance** to direct and coordinate mobilization planning within DOD and implements DOD responsibilities under the National Security Council national security emergency preparedness policy. **The MMG is the first level of mobilization planning.** It identifies mobilization responsibilities for DOD components and describes the tasks to be performed in peacetime and at the time of mobilization. It provides a common foundation for the preparation of detailed mobilization plans by the JS, Military Departments, and DOD agencies.

(3) **Mobilization planning is heavily influenced by the JSCP,** which tasks the CCDRs, their Service components, and the Military Departments to develop and refine OPLANs and supporting mobilization plans. **Another influence on mobilization planning is Department of Defense Instruction (DODI) 1225.06,** *Equipping the Reserve Forces,* which specifies DOD policy regardless of component.

b. **JPEC.** The JPEC collectively plans for the mobilization, deployment, employment, sustainment, redeployment, and demobilization of joint forces.

(1) **CJCS.** The CJCS, in consultation with the other members of the Joint Chiefs of Staff, **prepares integrated plans** for military mobilization, establishes planning relationships, develops mobilization options, and provides mobilization recommendations to SecDef. The CJCS also prepares and submits general strategic guidance for the development of industrial mobilization programs to SecDef, monitors the status and progress of mobilization, and prepares required reports for the President to submit to Congress. The Chairman of the Joint Chiefs of Staff Instruction (CJCSI) 3110.13, *Mobilization Guidance for the Joint Strategic Capabilities Plan,* establishes planning relationships.

(2) **JS.** The JS **supports CJCS** in integrating the mobilization plans of the Military Departments and DOD agencies. **The JS J-4 is the focal point in the JS** for integrating mobilization plans and coordinating mobilization execution. The mobilization responsibilities of the JS are shown in Figure III-1.

(3) **CCDRs.** The CCDRs **organize and employ assigned and attached forces** and are principally responsible for the **preparation of OPLANs and OPORDs.** They participate in the **development of national military and theater strategies** and participate in the **Planning, Programming, Budgeting, and Execution (PPBE) process** in addition to their operation planning responsibilities. As part of their operation planning responsibilities, CCDRs **identify and determine force and capability requirements,** including time phased force deployment data as a part of developing campaign plans, contingency plans, and joint OPORDs. The CCDRs are also responsible for identifying capability requirements of assigned RC forces and providing on-the-job training on theater-specific requirements when assigned forces are not on active duty or when they are on active duty for training. CCDRs normally will exercise training and readiness oversight (TRO) over assigned forces through Service component commanders.

For more information on TRO authority, see JP 1, Doctrine for the Armed Forces of the United States.

For more information on CCDR responsibilities specific to the RC, see Department of Defense Directive (DODD) 1235.10, Activation, Mobilization, and Demobilization of the Ready Reserve, *and DODI 1235.12,* Accessing the Reserve Components.

(a) **Supported CCDRs.** The JSCP or other joint operation planning authorities' task supported CCDRs to **prepare specific plans.** They **identify the capabilities needed** to support the plan; **time-phased requirements** for capabilities; and **capabilities needed** for reinforcement, deployment, and movement of the force, and for backfill of deployed capabilities. **This planning establishes the capabilities required and sustaining capabilities upon which supporting mobilization plans are based.** This planning requires extensive coordination among the supported CCDRs, supporting CCDRs, Services, and other involved USG departments and agencies. Supported CCDRs **request invocation of emergency mobilization authorities** when ordered to execute OPORDs requiring mobilization support.

JOINT STAFF MOBILIZATION RESPONSIBILITIES	
JOINT STAFF DIRECTORATE	**RESPONSIBILITIES**
Manpower and Personnel, J-1	Reviews manpower-related mobilization requirements.
	Identifies options for personnel augmentation, validates augmentation requests, and recommends appropriate authorities.
	Monitors the allocation and prioritization of inductees to the Services.
	Initiates manpower mobilization reporting for the Joint Staff during a crisis and serves as the Joint Staff point of contact for matters pertaining to manpower mobilization reporting policies and procedures.
Intelligence, J-2	Validates national intelligence augmentation support requirements for national intelligence support teams, quick reaction teams, and augmentation from national intelligence agencies that involve personnel or equipment.
Operations, J-3	Provides the combatant commander's requirements and the J-3's recommendation to the Chairman of the Joint Chiefs of Staff concerning the need for mobilizing Reserve Component units to support current operations.
	Presents alert and mobilization packages through the Chairman of the Joint Chiefs of Staff to the Secretary of Defense for final approval.
Logistics, J-4	Prepares alert and mobilization packages for submission to the Chairman of the Joint Chiefs of Staff, the Under Secretary of Defense for Personnel and Readiness, and the Secretary of Defense for approval.
	Determines the adequacy and feasibility of mobilization plans to support operation plans.
	Monitors the status and progress of mobilization and prepares required reports for submission by the President to Congress.
	Develops recommendations for the Chairman of the Joint Chiefs of Staff concerning the level of mobilization, emergency authorities required, and the need for induction under the Selective Service Act.
	Serves as the Joint Staff point of contact for matters pertaining to materiel and equipment, transportation, facilities, industrial base, health service support, and their impact on the environment and the economy.
	Develops joint mobilization doctrine, policies, procedures, and reporting instructions.
Strategic Plans and Policy, J-5	Prepares mobilization planning guidance for use by the combatant commanders and Services.
	Develops concepts for military mobilization to support strategic concepts and objectives.
	Prepares recommendations for declarations of national emergency and war.
Communications Systems, J-6	Through the Chairman of the Joint Chiefs of Staff provides Joint Staff position to the Office of the Secretary of Defense and the Military Departments concerning mobilization requirements for communications during mobilization.
	Ensures the design of command and control systems is capable of supporting the President, Secretary of Defense, Joint Staff, Military Departments, and combatant commanders during mobilization.
Joint Force Development, J-7	Supports the Chairman of the Joint Chiefs of Staff and the joint warfighter through joint force development (joint doctrine, training, education, lessons learned, capabilities, and assessments) in order to advance the operational effectiveness of the current and future joint force. As part of this responsibility, the J-7 plans, develops, and executes mobilization exercises.
Force Structure, Resources, and Assessment, J-8	Prepares joint mobilization estimates and studies.
	Serves as the Joint Staff point of contact concerning Active/Reserve Component mix and other force and resource development issues.
Joint Staff Legal Counsel	Serves as the Joint Staff point of contact for legal authorities pertaining to mobilization.
Assistants to the Chairman of the Joint Chiefs of Staff for National Guard Matters and Reserve Matters	Advise the Chairman of the Joint Chiefs of Staff on National Guard and reserve matters.

Figure III-1. Joint Staff Mobilization Responsibilities

(b) **Supporting CCDRs.** The JSCP or other joint planning authority task supporting CCDRs to **provide augmentation forces and other support** to designated supported CCDRs. **They may also require mobilized assets** to accomplish their respective support missions. Their supporting plans include mobilization requirements when appropriate. When needed, supporting CCDRs should request the mobilization of resources through the supported CCDR. As noted above, extensive coordination is required to ensure that all mobilization requirements are identified.

(4) **Military Departments and United States Coast Guard (USCG). The Military Departments provide forces and logistic support to the CCDRs** at the direction of SecDef. In peacetime, and until transferred to the Department of the Navy in time of war, the USCG serves under the control of the Secretary of Homeland Security (SECHS). USCG units under the Department of Homeland Security control may be assigned to a CCDR with the approval of SECHS. The Military Departments and the USCG **provide trained forces to the CCDRs.** They **prepare detailed mobilization plans** identifying the actual forces and support to be provided and **execute mobilization** at the direction of SecDef. Specifically, **the Secretaries of the Military Departments have the responsibilities shown in Figure III-2.**

(5) **DOD Agencies.** Six DOD agencies have significant responsibilities for supporting joint military mobilization. These are the Defense Information Systems Agency (DISA), Defense Logistics Agency (DLA), Defense Contract Management Agency (DCMA), Defense Finance and Accounting Service (DFAS), National Geospatial-Intelligence Agency (NGA), and Defense Health Agency. DISA and NGA receive operational direction from and report through CJCS to SecDef. The following paragraphs summarize the roles and responsibilities of each of these agencies in support of joint military mobilization.

(a) **DISA. DISA participates in all communications system mobilization planning activities.** DISA collects and analyzes the telecommunications requirements derived from these planning activities, and develops mobilization plans. **DISA modifies its**

Military Department Secretary Responsibilities

- Prepare military and industrial mobilization plans.

- Identify and request invocation of emergency authorities necessary to implement mobilization plans.

- Plan for the fill and sustainment of organized and/or structured units with all categories of personnel and equipment.

- Mobilize and demobilize their portion of the Reserve Component in crisis and war.

- Mobilize their civilian work force in crisis and war.

- Reorganize, reconstitute, and redeploy rotational forces during sustained crises and war.

Figure III-2. Military Department Secretary Responsibilities

mobilization plans, if required, and ensures the responsiveness of the Defense Communications System to the actual requirements of the President, OSD, JS, CCDRs, and Services. DISA also supports the National Communications System (NCS) and employs the nation's commercial communications resources to support defense requirements.

(b) **DLA.** Based on the Services' mobilization plans, **DLA develops plans to support the Military Departments and other authorized customers** with DLA-managed materiel and services. These plans include substantial industrial preparedness planning based on the CCDRs' critical item list (CIL) and extensive production base analysis conducted in coordination with OSD, the JS, and the Military Departments. Across the range of military operations, **DLA provides logistic support to the Services, advises the JS and CCDRs on the status of inventories of DLA-managed items,** and **recommends resource allocations and production priorities** when appropriate. DLA also has a disposal, reutilization, and marketing mission, and is responsible for the criteria and procedures for disposal of hazardous waste, excess property, scrap, and demilitarized property generated by DOD activities.

(c) **DCMA.** DCMA is the CSA that provides worldwide contract management services. With the Armed Forces' increased use of contractors in theaters, DCMA's role has become critical to formulating productive relationships with the JS, CCDRs, and senior acquisition executives to provide the best possible support.

(d) **DFAS. DFAS is the focal point for joint financial management issues.** DFAS works with the CCDRs to develop the financial management annexes to joint OPLANs. DFAS develops guidance regarding personnel pay issues, providing entitlement and tax information to members and dependents, and ensuring that the financial systems are able to support mobilization efforts. **DFAS formed a DFAS-wide crisis management system** to ensure that all DFAS crisis coordination centers are informed of financial management issues as they occur.

(e) **NGA.** In peacetime, **NGA develops and maintains mobilization plans to ensure continued geospatial intelligence (GEOINT) support** to joint forces under crisis and wartime conditions. NGA, in conjunction with DLA, provides the CCDRs with operational levels of geospatial information and services (GI&S) GEOINT products sufficient to meet initial mobilization requirements. In crisis and war, **NGA executes its plans and procedures for increased data collection** and increased production and distribution of its products.

(f) **Defense Health Agency.** The Defense Health Agency supports CCDRs by providing integrated delivery of shared services, functions, and activities to include the TRICARE Health Plan, pharmacy programs, medical education and training, medical research and development, health information technology (IT), health care facility planning, public health, medical logistics, acquisition, budget and resource management, and other common business and clinical processes.

For more discussion on GI&S and GEOINT, see JP 2-03, Geospatial Intelligence in Joint Operations.

c. **Joint Deployment Process Owner (JDPO) and the Distribution Process Owner (DPO).** The JS J-3 Joint Force Coordinator as the JDPO serves as the DOD focal point to improve the joint deployment process. USTRANSCOM supports the JS J-3 Joint Force Coordinator and other joint force providers during the planning and execution of the deployment and redeployment process. USTRANSCOM, as the DPO, provides the strategic distribution capability to move forces and materiel in support of JFC operational requirements and to return personnel, equipment, and materiel to home and/or demobilization stations. The JDPO and the DPO shall provide applicable guidance throughout the planning and deployment process.

For more information on the JDPO, see DODI 5158.05, Joint Deployment Process Owner, *and JP 3-35,* Deployment and Redeployment Operations.

d. **Mobilization Planner.** The role of the mobilization planner is to assist DOD, Service, and joint forces in developing policies and procedures required to activate and inactivate RC personnel under peacetime and crisis response conditions. The mobilization planner provides subject matter expertise on the sourcing and employment of RC forces in support of the planning and execution of joint plans and orders. The mobilization planner may be a DOD civilian or an RC member activated at the outset of a contingency to augment DOD, joint, Service, or CCMD staff, or may be an AC or RC subject matter expert already on staff. The mobilization planner performs various roles and tasks in supporting the mobilization and demobilization of RC personnel. The roles and tasks include reviewing and updating projected RC requirements; coordinating reporting requirements; determining sourcing of immediate manpower augmentation; reviewing mobilization plans, policies, and procedures; reviewing best practices and lessons learned from previous mobilizations; monitoring the mobilization process; and monitoring force assignments against requirements.

CHAPTER IV
RESOURCE AREAS

"Still unclear was the nation's willingness to learn the war's lessons about preparedness. It was plain that the materiel side of mobilization was the most costly, complex, and time consuming. The war (referring to World War I) Assistant Secretary of War Benedict Crowell said had 'upset the previous opinion that adequate military preparedness is largely a question of trained manpower.'"

Mobilization, Center for Military History Publication 72-32

1. Introduction

a. **Military mobilization requires the assembly and organization of resources** in 12 interdependent resource areas (legal authorities, funding, environment, manpower, materiel and equipment, transportation, facilities, industrial base, training base, health services, communications, host-nation support [HNS]). **Commanders and mobilization planners should understand the activities occurring in any one area may have an influence on each of the others.** Depending on the situation, activating additional manpower may generate requirements for additional industrial production, training base capacity, health services, communications support, and HNS.

b. **This chapter provides an overview of major mobilization activities by resource area.** The discussion in each resource area includes a **list of the providers of the resource, the options available to decision makers for using the resource,** and **the likely impact a mobilization decision made in one area could have on the other areas.**

c. Each of the 12 resource areas discussed in this chapter contributes to developing, expanding, sustaining, or positioning military capability so it may be applied to protect our national security interests in an emergency (see Figure IV-1). **Commanders and mobilization planners consider the impact of mobilization activities on the environment as well as the requirements of legal authorities and funding** to enable the timely execution of mobilization activities. The CCMDs, Services, and subordinate commands have an obligation to consider possible environmental effects with respect to construction, modernization, and other activities to facilitate mobilization and demobilization, to include obtaining environmental permits as required by applicable US law. Mobilization planners should also anticipate and plan for the impact of additional facility, training land, and range usage resulting from the influx of personnel and increased operating tempo. Lessons learned may provide useful information during planning. This section discusses, in turn, the sources of these enabling resources as well as the options available and actions necessary to obtain them.

For detailed discussion of joint lessons learned, see CJCSI 3150.25, Joint Lessons Learned Program.

REPRESENTATIVE MOBILIZATION ACTIONS IN RESOURCE AREAS	
RESOURCE AREA	**ACTION**
Legal Authorities	Requests to mobilize personnel generally require the identification of a specific level of emergency to trigger the applicable authority. Statutes providing emergency authority specify the level of emergency at which they can be invoked or implemented. Once invoked, the President may delegate his authority to lower levels.
Funding	It is necessary to ensure that sufficient funding is available for known obligations and may be necessary to seek additional appropriations or authorizing legislation to fund the mobilization. Supplemental funding requests should include all costs of training and equipping the force.
Environment	Mobilization planners must consider four categories of environmental statutes: compliance, clean-up, conservation, and impact analysis. The potential impact mobilization might have upon the environment should be identified and if compliance may not be possible, legal counsel should be engaged to determine possible options: negotiations, exemptions, waivers.
Manpower	Sources of military and civilian manpower for mobilization must be identified: Reserve Component (RC), military retirees, volunteers, civilians, contractors, etc. Three additional actions may be taken: stop-loss, stop-movement, and redistribution actions. Military manpower mobilization options are depicted in Figure IV-2. Impact of RC utilization on the economy and employers should be considered.
Materiel and Equipment	Planners must determine the need to increase the availability of materiel and equipment to accommodate the needs of a larger active force, and/or alleviate shortages by allocating or redistributing materiel and equipment in accordance with validated priorities. See Figure IV-3.
Transportation	Transportation mobilization options (intertheater and intratheater) must be identified, and the impact of augmenting intertheater air mobility, strategic sealift, and intra-continental United States (CONUS) transportation assets on other resource areas should be considered. See Figure IV-4.
Facilities	Sources of facilities to house, train, equip, and support personnel must be identified. Options for expanding facilities include reopening unused capacity, initiating emergency military construction projects, and acquiring new facilities. See Figure IV-5.
Industrial Base	Planners must consider the need and impacts for industrial base expansion and accelerated production. Options include expanding the industrial base, implementing the Defense Production Act, and obtaining allied production support. Additional legal authorities, environmental impacts, and funding may be required. See Figure IV-6.
Training Base	Planners must identify the requirement to expand the training base for non-prior Service personnel and reclassification and refresher training. This will additionally affect manpower, materiel and equipment, facilities, health services, and funding resource areas. See Figure IV-7.
Health Services	Theater required medical support, patient evacuation, and force health protection policies must be identified. Military mobilization plans should include provisions for activating RC health services professionals for theater medical support and hospital beds to meet additional health care requirements. Options include RC backfill and expanding the CONUS health services base. See Figure IV-8.
Communications	The Department of Homeland Security monitors and provides recommendations for the use of communications resources, and maintains liaison with commercial providers. The President can take immediate measure to ensure the continuous operation and security of telecommunications systems (Title 47, United States Code, Section 606).
Host-Nation Support	Department of State and Department of Defense must establish some form of mutual support, defense cooperation, and/or acquisition and cross-servicing agreements with US allies and friends. If agreements are not in place, new agreements must be developed.

Figure IV-1. Representative Mobilization Actions in Resource Areas

SECTION A. LEGAL AUTHORITIES

2. **Legal Authorities**

a. **Categories of Legal Authority. There is a broad range of legal authority that enables or limits mobilization and emergency actions.** Many of these authorities are available to the President in any level of emergency; others become available with a Presidential declaration of national emergency. Still others have been reserved by Congress pending passage of a public law or joint resolution of national emergency or declaration of war.

b. **Action Required to Invoke Legal Authorities. Statutes providing emergency authority specify the level of emergency at which they can be invoked and implemented.** Once invoked, the President may delegate authority to lower levels (e.g., SecDef, Secretaries of the Military Departments, CCDRs) (Title 3, USC, Section 301). As provided in the National Emergencies Act of 1976, Title 50, USC, Section 1631, **the President must specify the authority upon which he or other officers will act and such specification must be identified** in executive orders published in the Federal Register and transmitted to Congress. Requests to mobilize personnel generally require the identification of a specific level of emergency to trigger the applicable authority. For example, when mobilization requests are received from the Military Departments or CCDRs, the requests are integrated by the JS and forwarded with a draft executive order to SecDef as a recommendation for Presidential action. For various reasons, including international sensitivities and a policy goal of minimizing impacts upon RC members, major mobilization actions, such as involuntary personnel call-ups, are often conducted incrementally and may involve seeking legal authority on an incremental basis. **Failure to obtain the requested authority in a timely fashion could preclude or limit the desired activity in one or more resource areas.** Appendix A, "Legal Authorities," contains a more complete description of key legal authorities relative to mobilization.

MEMORANDUM FOR THE SECRETARIES OF THE MILITARY DEPARTMENTS, CHAIRMAN OF THE JOINT CHIEFS OF STAFF

SUBJECT: Partial Mobilization for World Trade Center and Pentagon Attacks

Pursuant to Section 12302 of Title 10 of the United States Code and the Executive Order 13223 of September 14, 2001, entitled "Ordering the Ready Reserve of the Armed Forces to Active Duty and Delegating Certain Authorities to the Secretary of Defense and the Secretary of Transportation," I hereby delegate to the Secretaries of the Military Departments authority to order to active duty Ready Reserve members as follows:

(1) Army: not more than 10,000 members of the Army Ready Reserve to provide combat support and combat service support.

(2) Navy and Marine Corps: not more than 3,000 members of the Naval Ready Reserve and not more than 7,500 members of the Marine Corps Ready Reserve.

---

(3) Air Force: not more than 13,000 members of the Air Force Ready Reserve.

The Secretaries of the Military Departments shall coordinate their exercise of the authority delegated by this memorandum with the Chairman of the Joint Chiefs of Staff or his designee.

The Secretaries of the Military Departments shall submit to me requests for additional authority to order Ready Reserve units and personnel to active duty as necessary, after coordination with the Chairman of the Joint Chiefs of Staff.

I hereby redelegate to the Secretaries of the Military Departments the President's authorities under Sections 123, 123a, 527, 12006, 12302, and 12305 of Title 10, United States Code. The authorities delegated by this memorandum may be redelegated to civilian subordinates who are appointed to their offices by the President, by and with the advice and consent of the Senate. The authorities granted herein may not be exercised to exceed general officer, field grade officer, and E-8 and E-9 enlisted personnel authorizations. The Assistant Secretary of Defense for Force Management Policy may issue such instructions consistent with the memorandum as may be necessary to ensure the effective implementation of this memorandum.

Donald Rumsfeld
Secretary of Defense
14 September 2001

SECTION B. FUNDING

3. Funding

a. **Funding considerations often require special attention.** To facilitate mobilization for unplanned military operations, it is necessary to ensure that sufficient funding is available for known obligations. At the outset of an operation, **senior decision makers should be aware of the magnitude of associated costs and recognize the possible impacts on other areas.** It may be necessary to seek additional appropriations or authorizing legislation to fund the mobilization. CJCS does not make funding decisions. In peacetime, CJCS assesses the impact of operational resource requests made by the Military Departments and DOD agencies in the PPBE process and recommends to SecDef how available funding should be distributed to implement the NMS. In wartime, CJCS, in consultation with the Joint Chiefs of Staff, may provide advice to the President and SecDef concerning funding priorities.

b. A **major mobilization will affect virtually all resource areas, well beyond the costs of salaries, benefits, and subsistence of the personnel involved.** Planners should include the costs of transportation, housing, health services, training, personnel security investigations, and equipping the force in estimating the total cost and supplemental or amended funding requests.

SECTION C. ENVIRONMENT

4. Environment

a. **General.** **The US has a substantial framework of environmental laws.** Awareness of environmental issues, requirements for compliance, and the liabilities or penalties associated with noncompliance mandate the identification and resolution of environmental issues that affect mobilization. It is DOD policy to comply with applicable environmental laws and regulations although national security exemptions may be available (DODI 4715.6, *Environmental Compliance*).

b. Mobilization activities, particularly as they relate to facilities, may trigger the need for an environmental assessment or an environmental impact statement. Mobilization planners should consult with staff legal counsel to determine whether planned activities constitute a major federal action or otherwise require specific actions under law. Impact analysis is conducted in accordance with the National Environmental Policy Act of 1969, Title 42, USC, Sections 4321-4361. It requires that major federal actions significantly affecting the quality of the human environment be preceded by a detailed statement by the responsible federal official. This statement identifies environmental effects of the proposed actions that cannot be avoided and alternatives to the proposed actions.

c. **Options for Obtaining Relief from Environmental Requirements**

(1) Planners should identify the potential impact that mobilization might have upon the environment in supporting mobilization plans and provide for compliance with applicable environmental laws. If it appears compliance may not be possible, planners should consult legal counsel to determine what, if any, options may be available. Possible options include negotiations with federal, state, and local agencies to develop acceptable alternative means of environmental protection; seeking a national security exemption under certain laws; and a request for legislation may be submitted to exempt critical industries and DOD organizations from regulatory requirements. Triggers should be established during mobilization planning so that the required environmental waivers can be prepared before training of mobilized forces is jeopardized during a crisis.

(2) Planning for actions to remedy damage caused as the result of waivers or noncompliance with environmental standards during mobilization should be taken as soon as possible. For example, additional military and civilian personnel with needed skills such as explosive ordnance disposal may be required to clean up the operational area.

(3) Response to no-notice emergencies and contingencies should not be delayed due to National Environmental Protection Act requirements. Documentation should take place as soon as possible.

For additional guidance on environmental considerations for operational planning, see JP 3-34, Joint Engineer Operations.

SECTION D. MANPOWER

5. Sources of Military Manpower

Manpower mobilization augments the peacetime AC military end strength. **Sources of military mobilization manpower include members of the RC, military retirees, volunteers with prior service, and nonprior service (NPS) personnel who volunteer.** These resources are organized by law to provide responsiveness in crises. Figure IV-2 associates these sources of manpower with manpower mobilization options and the actions required to initiate a call-up. The legal authorities required for the call-up of the various manpower pools are listed with the corresponding option. All personnel augmentation requirements should be identified, validated, and sourced either through the Service components or the JS/Military Departments.

> **Note:** Though legal authority allows Secretaries of the Military Departments to draw on Reserve Component (RC) forces (which include retirees) during times of crisis, the impact of transferring productive members of the civilian sector into the military must be carefully weighed. Commanders must prudently weigh their needs to support a crisis with RC members with the needs of the civilian sector and the impact on future RC readiness. An increasing reliance on the RC could eventually diminish employer and community support and thus RC participation.

6. Additional Military Manpower Mobilization Actions

In addition to the call-up of manpower from reserve and retiree manpower pools, **three other actions can be taken to ensure adequate manpower during mobilization.** These are stop-loss, stop-movement, and personnel redistribution actions. **Stop-loss actions** allow the Military Departments to retain personnel beyond their terms of service. Stop-movement actions refer to a number of policy and procedural actions that can be taken by the Military Departments to stabilize AC and RC personnel and ensure the maximum number are available for assignment to high-priority duties. These activities may include canceling temporary and permanent change of station travel, changing tour length policies, and curtailing attendance at Service schools. **Military Departments take internal redistribution actions** during a crisis to ensure that they maintain high-priority units at the highest level of personnel readiness until personnel fill and replacement pipeline throughput can be increased.

7. Civilian Manpower

Civilian manpower is an integral part of the DOD total joint force policy. Future crises will require careful management of the civilian work force.

MILITARY MANPOWER MOBILIZATION: SOURCES AND OPTIONS

SITUATION	SOURCES OF MANPOWER	MOBILIZATION OPTIONS	ACTION REQUIRED
Domestic emergency (e.g., natural disaster, civil disturbance)	Army National Guard and Air National Guard	Federalize National Guard troops under Title 10, United States Code (USC), Sections 12406 and 331-333	President publishes proclamation and an executive order.
	Army Reserve, Navy Reserve, Marine Corps Reserve, and Air Force Reserve	Call to active duty for up to 120 days under Title 10, USC, Section 12304a	Governor requests Federal Assistance for a major disaster or emergency, Secretary of Defense (SecDef) orders the mobilization, authority delegates to Secretaries of the Military Departments.
Any level of emergency (with or without a declared national emergency)	Volunteers from the National Guard and Reserve	Call for volunteers under Title 10, USC, Section 12301(d)	Secretaries of the Military Departments solicit volunteers with needed skills and publish call-up orders.
	Regular and Reserve retirees with 20+ years of active service	Recall retirees under Title 10, USC, Section 688(a)	Secretaries of the Military Departments publish call-up orders.
	Volunteer enlistees	Enlist qualified volunteers	Military Departments accept qualified applicants in accordance with Department of Defense and Service standards and policies.
	Selected Reserve - Units - Individual Mobilization Augmentees (IMAs)	Call to active duty up to 200,000 Selected Reservists (no more than 30,000 members of the Individual Ready Reserve [IRR]) under Title 10, USC, Section 12304 (Presidential Reserve Call-up)	President publishes executive order. Military Departments publish call-up orders based on SecDef implementing instructions. President must report to the Congress within 24 hours on anticipated use of forces.
		Call to active duty up to 60,000 Selected Reservists for not more than 365 consecutive days for a preplanned mission in support of a combatant command under Title 10, USC, Section 12304b	Secretary of the Military Department publish call-up orders and submit a report to Congress setting forth the circumstances necessitating the action. Manpower and associated costs must be specifically included and identified in the defense budget materials for appropriate fiscal year(s).
	Draftees	Initiate conscription	The President and SecDef request amendment to the Selective Service Act (Title 50, USC, Section 451) authorizing conscription.
War or national emergency	Ready Reserve - Units - IRRs - IMAs	Call to active duty up to 1,000,000 Ready Reservists for up to 24 months under Title 10, USC, Section 12302 (Partial Mobilization)	Presidential proclamation of a national emergency and an executive order (or congressional declaration of national emergency). Military Departments publish call-up orders based on SecDef implementing instructions.
	Remaining Ready Reserve - Retired Reserve - Standby Reserve	Call to active duty remaining Reserve Component personnel under Title 10, USC, Section 12301a (Full Mobilization)	Passage of legislation or a joint resolution of Congress declaring war or national emergency. Military Departments publish call-up orders.
	New units and personnel	Add new force structure and personnel necessary to achieve national security objectives (Total Mobilization)	Passage of legislation authorizing additional force structure and manpower.

Figure IV-2. Military Manpower Mobilization: Sources and Options

a. In theaters, USG service employees and contractors, with skills essential to support military missions, may remain after other US civilians and their families have been evacuated. The Services and DOD agencies designate these government service employees and contractors as emergency-essential and provide necessary training and other support for their crisis and wartime duties. Other government service employees and contractors with critical skills may deploy to the theater individually or with supported military units. The geographic combatant commander (GCC) determines admission requirements to the theater, and the respective Services and agencies implement those requirements for their employees. Some foreign-national civilian employees (local or third country nationals) may also remain to support the mission based on the need for their skills, level of danger, and agreements with the host country.

b. In the US, **the Services and DOD agencies reallocate incumbent civilian personnel from peacetime to the highest priority functions** through detailing, reassignment, and cross-training. When a crisis begins, the Services and agencies activate **recruiting area staffing committees** to find local solutions for meeting these requirements. Solutions can include:

(1) **Overtime** and extended workweek authorizations.

(2) Implementing plans for **replacing employees ordered to active duty** because of RC or retired-military obligations.

(3) Using **civilian retirees** and **retired military personnel** not expected to be recalled.

(4) Using **employees on loan** from other federal, state, or local agencies.

(5) Using **contractors.**

(6) Allocation of **new employees** after hiring.

(7) Activating applicable crisis procedures with Office of Personnel Management regional offices and with state and local employment offices to **provide required applicants on an expedited basis.**

8. Manpower Mobilization Options

a. **Manpower mobilization options provide great flexibility to the President and SecDef for responding to a crisis.** Response levels are tied to the legal authorities available before a Presidential declaration of national emergency or a congressional declaration of national emergency or war as shown in Figure IV-2 and Figure I-1. **Before a declaration of national emergency, the Secretaries of the Military Departments can call for RC volunteers** who have needed skills and activate them for short periods of time. RC volunteers were used effectively during Operation ALLIED FORCE in Kosovo and Operation ENDURING FREEDOM in Afghanistan. In addition, both volunteer reservists and recalled retirees were used during Operation IRAQI FREEDOM in Iraq. **Secretaries of the Military Departments can involuntarily mobilize up to 60,000 members of the Selected Reserve up to 365 consecutive days to augment active forces for preplanned and prebudgeted missions in support of a CCMD per Title 10, USC, Section 12304b. The budget information on such costs must include a description of the mission for which such units are anticipated to be ordered to active duty and the anticipated length of time of the order of such units to active duty on an involuntary basis. PRC authority makes up to 200,000 members of the Selected Reserve (including up to 30,000 Individual Ready Reserve [IRR] members) available for involuntary activation for up to 365 consecutive days in support of a named operational mission per Title 10, USC,**

Section 12304. This authority was used effectively to mobilize Air and Army National Guard units during Operation DESERT SHIELD/DESERT STORM and during operations in Haiti. This authority can be used to send a strong signal of US resolve to friends and foes alike and can serve as a prelude to partial mobilization. **When a governor requests federal assistance in responding to a major disaster or emergency, SecDef may order any member of the Army Reserve, Navy Reserve, Marine Corps Reserve, and Air Force Reserve to involuntary active duty up to 120 days per Title 10, USC, Section 12304a.** This authority was used effectively to assist with Hurricane Sandy. **A Presidential declaration of national emergency and invocation of the partial mobilization authority makes up to one million members of the Ready Reserve available for up to 24 consecutive months per Title 10, USC, Section 12302.** This partial mobilization authority includes members of the IRR, which is an additional source of trained manpower to be used as Service needs dictate. Like the PRC, activations under this authority can be made incrementally or all at once to meet the needs of the crisis as it develops. **Full mobilization may be ordered in time of war or national emergency declared by Congress or when otherwise authorized by law per Title 10, USC, Section 12301(a).** Under full mobilization the Retired and Standby Reserves become available, as well as Ready Reserves not called previously. **Manpower requirements** for force expansion beyond the peacetime-authorized force structure and sustainment in a protracted conflict **may require legislation authorizing activation of the Selective Service System (SSS)** for the conscription of additional forces. Some retirees are available for recall during all levels of mobilization per Title 10, USC, Sections 688(a), 690(c), and 12307.

b. Although volunteerism is important, the mobilization planner should be judicious in exercising this course of action (COA). The use of RC volunteers is very attractive because they can fill PRC billets, but do not count against the Service's PRC personnel cap for tours of 365 days or less. As such, the use of volunteers can add significantly to a Service's ability to meet the ever-increasing requirement to support peacetime commitments and ongoing operations. However, excessive use of volunteers removes personnel from RC units, which could result in a reduction of the unit's readiness in the event of unit mobilization. Individual voluntary reserve participation affects the availability of the member in a mobilization augmentation role. Another condition mobilization planners must take into account is SecDef's dwell time policy which establishes the length of time RC units should not be mobilized after demobilizing from a prior mobilization/call-up.

For information on dwell time, see DODD 1235.10, Activation, Mobilization, and Demobilization of the Ready Reserve, *and DODI 1235.12,* Accessing the Reserve Component (RC).

9. **Impact of Manpower Mobilization and Activation on Other Resource Areas**

a. **Selected Reserve Manpower. Mobilized Selected Reserve units create time-phased demands for all classes of supply,** especially rations, fuel, and ammunition; major items of equipment; and repair parts. They also create temporary, but significant, **demands for intra-CONUS transportation** as they move from home stations to marshalling areas for reception, staging, onward movement, and integration with the gaining force commander. **The RC is an economical contribution to the force mix;**

however, planners must anticipate the cost of adequate housing and proper outfitting of the RC in a contingency. They create increased **workloads at existing facilities** for personnel support, energy, housing, training areas, and storage and may require construction of new facilities. They create **demands for additional industrial base output** of all classes of consumables and for major end items when war reserve stocks are depleted. Mobilized Selected Reserve units and personnel may impose **additional demands on the training base** if some unit members are unskilled or have not completed mandatory training. They may create **significant demands** on health services as they mobilize. Dependents of RC members will also impose **additional workloads on CONUS base support services and health care resources.**

b. **Individual Augmentees (IAs).** The two categories of IA are individual Service augmentee (ISA) or a joint individual augmentee (JIA). IAs can be used to fill shortages or when an individual with specialized knowledge or skill sets is required. As a result, IAs can include members from an entirely different branch of service. The current IA system works on a combination of ordered and volunteer assignments mirroring manning requirements. An ISA is an individual augment sourced internally within the Service to meet Service-specific requirements and tasks. It is a position established and validated under approved Service procedures for the purpose of satisfying a grouping of tasks, capable of being performed by one individual, for whom no authorized position has been established in the unit's manning documents. A JIA is an unfunded temporary manpower requirement (or member filling an unfunded temporary manpower position) identified on a joint manning document by a supported CCDR to augment joint force staff operations during contingencies. A JIA will fill joint force headquarters requirements; tactical-level deployment is not appropriate for JIA sourcing. Sourcing by JIA is meant to be the last method for obtaining manpower for positions. This includes positions at permanent organizations required to satisfy an elevated mission in direct support of contingency operations. Aside from mandated personal protective equipment, JIAs will not deploy with additional equipment. Neither collective team training nor specialized training exceeding one-two weeks should be needed. Either AC or RC or DOD civilian personnel can fill JIA positions. Individual mobilization augmentees (IMAs) filling, or activated to fill, their IMA billets are not considered a JIA.

c. **Considerations for IAs.** Individuals mobilized from the various sources (IRR, military retirees, and Standby Reserve) place the same demands on other resource areas, as described above for Selected Reserve manpower, once they report to their assigned units. Before they are assigned to a unit, however, they create **demands for intra-CONUS transportation;** for an **initial issue of clothing and individual equipment;** and for **subsistence, housing, and health care.** Most individuals mobilized as IAs will need **reclassification** or **refresher training** at the training base, placing unique timeliness demands on the organizations tasked with processing and training. If assigned overseas for unit backfill or as replacements, they will place a **demand for a nonunit personnel space** on the strategic transportation system and require weapons, ammunition, and mobility bags.

d. **NPS Manpower.** NPS manpower (draftees and volunteers) imposes essentially the same demands as IA imposes on the other resource areas. **Because they are**

untrained at accession, they will impose demands on the training base for basic and initial skills training.

e. **Civilian Manpower.** Civilian personnel create demands on resource areas based on their employment categories. **DOD civilian employees at military installations** normally live at home and require only a salary and workspace to do their jobs. **A DOD civilian or contractor employee required in the theater** may require clothing; chemical, biological, radiological, and nuclear defense equipment and training; passports and visas; housing and subsistence; intra-CONUS, intertheater, and intratheater transportation; combat skills; survival, evasion, resistance, and escape training; and health services, as well as becoming an additional force protection consideration. The use of DOD civilian and contractor personnel or local nationals frees military personnel to perform operational vice ancillary supporting tasks. DOD civilians, along with system support and external support contractors, are often used to augment military forces in noncombat operations. Sometimes, these personnel have critical skills that are lacking in the Services. The **Logistics Civil Augmentation Program** provides contingency support to augment Army force structure. The **Air Force Contract Augmentation Program and global contingency construction** provide contingency support for the Air Force and Navy, respectively.

For additional guidance on operational contracting considerations, see JP 4-10, Operational Contract Support.

f. **Civilian Expeditionary Workforce (CEW).** The CEW program provides a pre-identified source of civilian manpower to support DOD combat operations, contingencies, emergencies, humanitarian missions, and other expeditionary requirements. The CEW is both position-based and person-based facilitating the organizing, training, and equipping of civilians for rapid response and quick assimilation into new operational environments.

10. Employer and Community Support

The success of the nation's defense is dependent on the availability of highly trained members of the total force. **DOD has assigned the National Committee of Employer Support for the Guard and Reserve (NCESGR) the responsibility of promoting both public and private understanding of the National Guard and reserve in order to gain US employer and community support. This is accomplished through programs, personnel policies, and practices that encourage employee and citizen participation in the National Guard and reserve programs.** NCESGR's mission is to obtain employer and community support to ensure the availability and readiness of reserve/guard forces. Among their many responsibilities, the NCESGR assists in preventing, resolving, and/or reducing employer and employee problems and misunderstandings that result from National Guard or reserve membership, training, and duty requirements. This is accomplished through information services and informal mediation as well as assisting in the education of National Guard and reserve members with respect to their obligations and responsibilities to employers. This resource is available to military leaders, employers, and reservists in resolving issues impeding rapid and effective mobilization.

a. **Impact of RC Utilization on the Economy and Community.** Community support is crucial to maintaining a viable source of military manpower—RC personnel. **Mobilization impacts the economy, employers, and the community.** Commanders and mobilization planners should be aware that the call-ups may impact key national economic segments. Critical economic segments closely related to RC call-ups include communications, transportation (especially airline services), and public services (e.g., police, fire, and medical).

b. Throughout the mobilization process and prior to release from active duty, RC members will be provided with transition assistance services in accordance with DODD 1332.35, *Transition Assistance for Military Personnel,* and employment outreach services as described in Public Law 112-56, *Veterans Opportunity to Work to Hire Heroes Act of 2011.*

c. The Military Department Secretary should not use RC call-ups as a long-term fix to active duty force structure shortfalls unrelated to the call-up contingency. It must be remembered that continued reliance on the RC requires the transferring of productive members of the economy and community into the military, which may result in diminished employer and community support over time, thus adversely impacting RC readiness and retention.

SECTION E. MATERIEL AND EQUIPMENT

11. Sources of Materiel and Equipment

The materiel and equipment resource area includes all classes of supply. It includes equipment on hand in units, remain-behind equipment in theater, war reserves, pre-positioned equipment, and the output of the depot maintenance system and industrial base. Additional sources include items in the security assistance pipelines and off-the-shelf items from domestic and foreign commercial sources. **These sources and the options and actions for obtaining them are listed in Figure IV-3.**

MATERIEL AND EQUIPMENT MOBILIZATION: SOURCES AND OPTIONS		
SOURCES OF MATERIEL AND EQUIPMENT	MOBILIZATION OPTIONS	ACTION REQUIRED
Continental United States/in-theater equipment on hand in units	Redistribution based on emergency priorities	Military Department decisions based on supported commanders' requirements and priorities.
War reserve and pre-positioned stockpiles	Release stocks	Military Department decisions for retail items. Joint Materiel Priorities and Allocation Board decisions for wholesale stocks insufficient to meet demands of all claimants.
Depot system	Accelerate output	Military Department decisions based on supported commanders' requirements and priorities.
Industrial base	Accelerate output	Military Departments and Department of Defense agencies act to surge production of needed materiel and equipment.
Materiel and equipment in security assistance pipelines	Divert needed equipment from security assistance pipelines	The President and Secretary of Defense decision based on a determination that national security requirements outweigh political consequences.
Domestic and foreign commercial vendors	Purchase off-the-shelf products that meet military requirements	Military Department and Department of Defense agency decisions based on Federal acquisition regulations.

Figure IV-3. Materiel and Equipment Mobilization: Sources and Options

12. Materiel and Equipment Mobilization Options

Materiel and equipment mobilization consists of many activities that can be grouped under two major tasks: **increasing the availability of materiel and equipment** to accommodate the needs of a larger active force, and alleviating shortages by **allocating or redistributing materiel and equipment in accordance with validated priorities.** These activities can be undertaken either separately or in combination.

a. **Increasing Materiel and Equipment Availability.** Decision options that increase materiel and equipment availability include the release of war reserve and depot stocks, accelerating the output of the depot maintenance system, diverting items from foreign military sales and other security assistance programs, accelerating production rates of existing contracts for items like clothing, ammunition, vehicles and combat systems, rations, and procurement of commercial substitutes from domestic or foreign sources. **Each of these actions increases the number of items in the supply pipeline.** Except for the diversion of items earmarked for security assistance programs, these options are exercised by the Military Departments, DLA, and other DOD agencies as they provide for the logistic needs of their forces assigned to the CCDRs. **Action to divert items from security assistance programs** could have a significant impact on our relations with affected allies. This decision should follow discussions with the Department of State, specific chiefs of mission and country teams, and **the President or SecDef.** However, once diverted and allocated to a Military Department, they are distributed as determined by the owning Military Department.

b. **Allocating Materiel and Equipment Shortages. Shortages of Service-unique items are resolved by priority and allocation decisions** made internally by the Military Departments based on OPLAN priorities, and guided by DOD policy to equip earlier deploying units before those scheduled to deploy later, regardless of Service component. When confronted with a materiel or equipment shortage common to two or more US military claimants, SecDef, with the advice of CJCS, **determines priorities among the Services. The Joint Materiel Priorities and Allocation Board (JMPAB) executes this responsibility.** The JMPAB is chaired by the JS J-4 and includes other JS directors as well as general or flag officer representatives from the Military Departments. In multinational operations, the US may be responsible for providing significant materiel and equipment support to one or more allies or coalition partners. When shortages occur, **priority and allocation decisions for resolving conflicts among multinational partners, or between US claimants and multinational partners, are made by SecDef.**

SECTION F. TRANSPORTATION

13. Sources of Mobilization Transportation

Transportation resources are required to support mobilization, deployment, employment, sustainment, redeployment, and demobilization operations. Mobilization activities are supported principally by intra-CONUS air, rail, highway, pipeline, port facilities, and inland waterway assets of commercial firms. **These assets move units and unit equipment** through the mobilization process from home stations to marshalling areas to ports of embarkation; **IAs** from their homes to reception and training sites and then to replacement centers and ports of embarkation; and **individual issue equipment** from production and storage sites to ports of embarkation. **Deployment, employment, sustainment, and redeployment operations are supported primarily by intertheater airlift and sealift,** which move units, non-unit personnel, and sustainment items (non-unit equipment and supplies) from the US to the theaters. **RC transportation terminal units** provide the military interface at commercial seaports of embarkation, **deployment support units** assist with loading the equipment on commercial transportation, and **port security companies** provide security at military ocean terminals. **In many cases, these units are mobilized early to support deployment from CONUS.** The sources of additional transportation resources for mobilization and the options for mobilizing them are listed in Figure IV-4. **In some situations, additional transportation assets may be required before substantial deployments can be executed.**

See JP 3-35, Deployment and Redeployment Operations, *for further information on deployment and redeployment.*

14. Transportation Mobilization Options

A variety of options are available for mobilization of intertheater and intratheater airlift assets. Air Mobility Command assets can quickly be expanded by the **Air National Guard, Air Force Reserves,** and the **airlift assets of the US Navy Reserve. Additionally, the fleet can be augmented via contract commercial charters, and through the Civil Reserve Air Fleet.** Similarly, Military Sealift Command assets can also be quickly expanded by vessels activated from the Maritime Administration Ready Reserve Force (MARAD RRF) and by chartering US flag and foreign flag commercial vessels. **After activation of the MARAD RRF, additional ships can be activated from the National Defense Reserve Fleet to fill additional requirements for sealift.** Additional sealift sources detailed in Figure IV-4, such as the Voluntary Intermodal Sealift Agreement, the Voluntary Tanker Agreement, and requisitioning, may also be available.

15. Impact of Transportation Mobilization on Other Resource Areas

Mobilization of transportation resources will substantially affect the manpower resource area because highly skilled operators and crews are required, as well as maintenance cargo handling, and security personnel, at ports and trans-shipment points. The impact **of mobilized transportation resources** on **ports, airfields, highways, pipelines, railroads, and inland waterways; facilities** required for activation, maintenance, and storage; and **repair parts and materials handling equipment** may be significant. **Legal authorities and funding** are required to enable transportation resource expansion. Influence on the **training base** could be significant in a protracted conflict with high attrition rates of operator or crew personnel.

TRANSPORTATION MOBILIZATION: SOURCES AND OPTIONS		
SOURCES OF TRANSPORTATION AUGMENTATION	TRANSPORTATION MOBILIZATION OPTIONS	ACTIONS REQUIRED
ANY LEVEL Of EMERGENCY		
Strategic Airlift		
Reserve Component air mobility assets	Task Air Mobility Command, gained, Air Reserve Component, and Naval Reserve assets	Secretaries of the Air Force and Navy activate units and individuals with an appropriate call-up order.
Voluntary charter	Charter available commercial aircraft	Commander, United States Transportation Command (CDRUSTRANSCOM) obtains commercial charter aircraft.
Civil Reserve Air Fleet (CRAF) Stage I	Activate when required to augment capacity	CDRUSTRANSCOM activates and operationally directs Civil Reserve Air Fleet (CRAF) I assets with Secretary of Defense (SecDef) approval.
CRAF Stage II	Activate when required to augment capacity	CDRUSTRANSCOM activates and operationally directs CRAF II assets with SecDef approval.
Strategic Sealift		
Commercial sealift	Utilize available commercial vessels when required to augment United States Transportation Command controlled fleet	CDRUSTRANSCOM obtains commercial shipping.
Department of Defense (DOD) reduced operational status ships	Activate when required to augment sealift capacity	CDRUSTRANSCOM activates as required.
Ready Reserve Force	CDRUSTRANSCOM activates as delegated by SecDef	CDRUSTRANSCOM requests through Chairman of the Joint Chiefs of Staff (CJCS); SecDef approves by agreement with the Secretary of Transportation (SECTRANS); Maritime Administration (National Defense Reserve Fleet) implements.
Voluntary Intermodal Sealift Agreement (VISA)	Activate when required to augment sealift capacity	CDRUSTRANSCOM, with approval of SecDef, activates VISA with concurrence of SECTRANS.
Voluntary tanker agreement	Activate when required to augment sealift (tanker) capacity	CDRUSTRANSCOM activates as required.
Continental United States (CONUS) Transportation		
Commercial air, rail, highway, barge, transportation terminal unit	Activate the contingency response program. Mobilize seaport of embarkation transportation terminal units	The contingency response program team assembles at the call of CDRUSTRANSCOM to prevent or resolve transportation shortfalls. Secretary of the Army publishes call-up order for transportation terminal units.
NATIONAL EMERGENCY OR WAR		
Strategic Airlift		
CRAF Stage III	Activate when necessary to augment airlift capacity	CDRUSTRANSCOM activates and commands CRAF III assets with the approval of SecDef.
Foreign voluntary charters	Charter available foreign aircraft	CDRUSTRANSCOM enters into agreements with foreign carriers consistent with the Fly American Act.

North Atlantic Treaty Organization (NATO) Allied Pre-committed Civil Aircraft Program aircraft	Request NATO resources when required to augment US airlift capacity	North Atlantic Council requests reinforcements and responds to requests for airlift.
Strategic Sealift		
Requisitioned US-flag and effective US-controlled shipping vessels	Requisitioned as required to meet sealift requirements	With declaration of national emergency, SECTRANS requisitions ships at the request of SecDef.
Naval Inactive Fleet of the National Defense Reserve Fleet	Activate when required to augment sealift capacity	With declaration of national emergency, CDRUSTRANSCOM requests through CJCS; SecDef orders activation.
CONUS Transportation		
Air, rail, highway, and barge	Seek priorities and allocations of domestic transportation when required to augment capacity	With declaration of national emergency, the President invokes priorities and allocations for DOD.

Figure IV-4. Transportation Mobilization: Sources and Options

a. **Augmenting Intertheater Air Mobility. Each additional aircraft affects runway, throughput, marshalling, and temporary storage capacity at airfields.** These factors could become constraints at departure, en route, and arrival airfields. **Aircrews require subsistence and transient quarters,** and aircrew shortages and crew rest considerations could also become constraints. Influence on the military training base should be minimal unless commercial carriers lose their capability to conduct their respective training. **Some additional demands will be placed on the industrial base** as stocks of repair parts are depleted. Shortages of aviation fuel, lubricants, repair parts, hull and liability insurance, and qualified mechanics could become constraints.

b. **Augmenting Strategic Sealift.** In addition to applicable constraints listed above, **the charter, requisition, or activation of each additional ship draws on the available pool of licensed officers and certified merchant seamen.** The withdrawal of commercial vessel insurance and war-risk exclusion for crew life insurance may also constrain the use of commercial vessels. To surmount this constraint, the President may authorize SecDef, acting through the Secretary of Transportation, to issue war-risk insurance under Title XII of the Merchant Marine Act of 1936 (Title 46, USC, Section 1285). Additionally, Title 46, USC, Section 8103(g) requires that deck and engineer officers, if eligible, be a member of the Navy Reserve if serving on vessels on which an operating differential subsidy is paid, or on vessels (except a vessel of the Coast Guard or Saint Lawrence Seaway Development Corporation) owned or operated by the Department of Transportation (DOT) or by a corporation organized or controlled by the DOT. **Crew shortages could become a constraint,** particularly if market forces and mortality rates result in a reduced pool of available private sector US merchant mariners. Also, pulling ships from normal commercial service can have adverse long-term impacts on the commercial sealift carrier's business. **Ships require berthing and anchorage space at ports,** which, together with temporary storage, staging areas, cargo handling capabilities, and transportation mode links, determine throughput capacity. Laws governing the handling of hazardous materials, such as ammunition, limit the number of ports that can handle such loads. **Dry docks, shipyard facilities, and skilled labor are required** for activation and periodic refitting. Constraints in the other resource areas should be minimal except in extreme conditions marked by high attrition. Additionally, **shortages of stevedores** may be experienced if heavy demands are placed on multiple commercial ports within the same geographic area.

    c. **Augmenting Intra-CONUS Transportation Resources. DOD can request that DOT issue priority service or allocation orders to the commercial transportation industry to support DOD requirements.** Demands in the other resource areas should not be significant, except in extreme circumstances. Spot shortages in operator, crew, or maintenance personnel could occur if large numbers of commercial carrier employees are ordered to military duty or if local transportation demands are heavy. Spot shortages of fuel, repair parts, maintenance, and trans-shipment facilities could also occur during peak periods. At some installations, capacity of railheads and spurs could be a constraint.

    d. **Service-Unique Self-Deployment.** Planners should keep in mind that some Service personnel/units (e.g., combat aircraft and aircrews) deploy to theater on board their own warfighting equipment. Sometimes combat aircraft carry a full load of weapons and/or support equipment and crew members.

SECTION G. FACILITIES

16. Sources of Facilities

    DOD uses a wide variety of facilities to house, train, equip, and support personnel. Facilities also provide storage, maintain equipment, and conduct operations. Military bases, depots, medical treatment facilities, airfields, and seaports are representative examples. **Facilities with the capacity for supporting increased workloads during mobilization are obtained from the following sources: commercial facilities** that support DOD in peacetime; **unused and standby capacity** at existing government facilities; and new capacity developed on property acquired by DOD through lease, purchase, or exercise of other legal means. These are listed in Figure IV-5, together with the options and actions for acquiring needed facilities during mobilization.

FACILITY MOBILIZATION: SOURCES AND OPTIONS			
SITUATION	SOURCES OF FACILITIES	FACILITIES MOBILIZATION OPTIONS	ACTIONS REQUIRED
Any level of emergency	Existing government property		
	Standby capacity	Activate standby capacity	Military Departments act within available funding
	Unused capacity	Develop unused capacity	Military Departments initiate emergency military construction projects using unobligated funds (Title 10, United States Code [USC], Section 2803) or Secretary of Defense (SecDef) Contingency Construction Authority (Title 10, USC, Section 2804)
	Newly acquired property	Lease, purchase, and develop as required	
		Optimize supply chain management to minimize facility requirement	
National emergency or war	Existing government property	Develop unused capacity	Military Departments initiate emergency military construction projects with additional authorities available upon declaration of national emergency

	Newly acquired property	Lease, purchase, and develop as required	SecDef authorizes modifications to current military construction program within military construction appropriations and unobligated family housing funding (Title 10, USC, Section 2808)
	Recaptured former government property	Recapture and develop as provided by law	SecDef acts under statutory provisions for recapture of specified parcels of former federal property

Figure IV-5. Facility Mobilization: Sources and Options

17. Facilities Mobilization Options

Options for expanding facilities during mobilization include reopening unused capacity with actions short of new construction, **initiating emergency military construction projects** to increase capacity at existing facilities, **and acquisition of new facilities** through the recapture of former federal property. Facilities can include all kinds of military installations, airfields, and seaports in and outside CONUS.

a. **Initiate Emergency Military Construction. SecDef and Secretaries of the Military Departments can initiate emergency military construction projects** with unobligated balances of military construction funds, the SecDef contingency construction authority, or with a modified military construction program, enabled with a declaration of national emergency and unobligated military construction and family housing funds. Beyond these options, construction of new or expanded facilities requires a request for a supplemental military construction appropriation. Waivers or relief from environmental protection statutes and some occupational health and safety regulations may need to be requested through the appropriate chain of command.

b. **Acquire Additional Real Property and Commercial Facilities.** Under the law, hundreds of parcels of former federal property may be reacquired to provide land and improved infrastructure for conversion into needed facilities. In addition, privately owned lands may be acquired by condemnation for defense purposes, such as training or manufacturing of ammunition and other materiel. Reacquiring ex-federal property must be handled in accordance with applicable federal and military regulations before use, and this process may take some significant time and effort. For example, an environmental baseline survey will be needed to determine the condition of the property to be acquired.

18. Impact of Facilities Mobilization on Other Resource Areas

Expanding facilities will require more manpower, both military and civilian, to staff tenant organizations and provide required services. The greatest impact will be on the civilian side in the form of contract construction workers and DOD personnel employed to expand tenant support services. Host-nation civilians will provide the bulk of this support overseas. **There will be a significant local demand for construction materials and equipment**—from stocks and from the industrial base. As the facility grows in capacity or expands operations, **the increased population will require more health services and other support services.** If these resources are available, the impact on planned facilities expansion will be minimal. **Shortfalls in these areas will reduce capacity and constrain productivity.**

SECTION H. INDUSTRIAL BASE

19. Industrial Mobilization Sources

The US industrial base includes commercial production facilities and government-owned facilities. Some of the government-owned facilities are government-operated and some are contractor-operated. **Foreign producers of essential components, parts, and ammunition are included,** because foreign producers may be the only source for components of major equipment items. Because of the unique relationship existing between the US and Canada, the Canadian defense industry is recognized as part of a single North American defense industrial base. **The capabilities of Canadian industry may be included in US industrial preparedness planning.** Figure IV-6 lists these sources together with the options and actions required to expand their output.

INDUSTRIAL MOBILIZATION: SOURCES AND OPTIONS		
INDUSTRIAL BASE SOURCES	INDUSTRIAL MOBILIZATION OPTIONS	ACTIONS REQUIRED
DOMESTIC INDUSTRY		
Commercial producers of goods and services	Accelerate production from current sources of goods and services	Military Departments and Defense Logistics Agency contract for accelerated production from current producers of materiel based on planned or actual consumption rates and prioritized requirements of the combatant commanders.
	Expand production base capacity	Using the Defense Priorities and Allocation System (DPAS), Title 50, United States Code, Section 2071, obtain priority performance on Department of Defense contracts and orders.
		Using DPAS authorities and streamlined acquisition procedures, increase industrial capacity for production of materiel and equipment required to sustain the mobilized force.
DEFENSE INDUSTRIAL BASE		
Government-owned/government-operated production facilities	Primary industrial base to support peacetime training, deployment, contingency operations, war, peacekeeping, antiterrorism, homeland defense, and to protect and secure the US forces' technological advantage against our adversaries. This encompasses foreign military sales and other service support.	Accelerate production rates or activate standby and laid-away production capacity at government-owned/government-operated facilities and government-owned/contractor-operated facilities.
Government-owned/contractor-operated production facilities	See above	
FOREIGN INDUSTRY		
Commercial producers of goods and services		Seek additional production from foreign suppliers.

Figure IV-6. Industrial Mobilization: Sources and Options

20. Industrial Mobilization Options

Industrial base expansion includes actions to **accelerate production** within the existing industrial infrastructure, **add new production lines and factories,** and **implement provisions of the Defense Priorities and Allocation System (DPAS).** Because many components of key military items of equipment are now procured from foreign sources, increased emergency procurement from these sources has become, of necessity, a major industrial mobilization option.

21. Impact of Industrial Mobilization on the Other Resource Areas

a. **Expand the Industrial Base.** Surge production and industrial base expansion will require additional skilled manpower from the non-defense sectors of the national economy. **Local manpower shortages could develop** in areas hardest hit by extensive military manpower mobilization and competition between DOD contractors and others for limited numbers of the same skills. **Materiel and equipment stocks, transportation, and facilities could be significantly affected** if raw materials, finished products, tools, and test equipment become short; local and long distance hauling is not sufficiently manned; and new construction does not meet the demand. **Additional legal authorities may be invoked or requested** from Congress upon the determination that DOD production in a crisis is being adversely affected. **Environmental and occupational health and safety regulations may also require waivers.** Substantial additional funding may be required to enable increased production.

b. **Implement the DPAS.** The DPAS is authorized by the Defense Production Act (Title 50, USC, Section 2071) and **allows preferential treatment for contracts or orders relating to certain approved defense or energy programs** for military production and construction, military assistance to any foreign nation, and stockpiling. This authority specifically includes reordering national priorities and rationing available industrial resources (articles, materials, services, and facilities, including construction materials). The Department of Commerce is responsible for DPAS activities concerning industrial resources. Accordingly, DOD will coordinate with the Department of Commerce concerning industrial resource issues requiring resolution through DPAS.

c. **Obtain Allied Production Support. DOD has become increasingly reliant on foreign production** of essential components, repair parts, tools, and test equipment needed for domestic production of virtually all major weapons systems and other key items of materiel and equipment. Wartime surge and industrial base expansion can be expected to have a significant impact on foreign producers as well. **The reliability of these sources could significantly influence the ability to provide needed materiel and equipment to support and sustain operations.** Conversely, the availability of foreign production support in areas where the domestic production base can no longer expand could have substantial positive results on the manpower, materiel and equipment, and facilities resource areas. Similar to domestic source problems, foreign supplier problems should be forwarded through the DPAS chain for resolution by OSD and the Department of Commerce.

SECTION I. TRAINING BASE

22. Sources and Options for Expanding Training Base Capacity

The Services expand their institutional training bases to train NPS personnel to support and sustain an expanded force structure. **The training base also provides reclassification and refresher training** for IAs who need it. Based on the rate of force expansion and attrition due to casualties, disease, and nonbattle injuries, **training base output requirements are determined by the Services and compared to available capacity.** If there is a shortfall, additional capacity is added by mobilizing additional training organizations from the RC, by hiring DOD civilian employees, and by contracting for additional instructors and other training resources from the private sector. Sources, options, and actions for expanding training base capacity are listed in Figure IV-7.

EXPANDING TRAINING BASE CAPACITY: SOURCES AND OPTIONS			
SITUATION	SOURCES OF ADDITIONAL TRAINING BASE CAPACITY	TRAINING BASE EXPANSION OPTIONS	ACTIONS REQUIRED
Any level of emergency			Military Departments act to expand their institutional training establishments.
	Wartime policies and programs of instruction	Implement wartime training policies and programs	Implement wartime programs of instruction; extend the training day and training week; increase class size.
	Reserve Component (RC) training units	Expand existing training centers and schools	Call-up RC training base augmentation units as required.
	New training centers and schools	Add new training centers and schools	Call-up remaining RC training base augmentation units; activate new training units; acquire new training facilities and support.

Figure IV-7. Expanding Training Base Capacity: Sources and Options

23. Impact of Training Base Expansion on Other Resource Areas

Training base expansion may have significant impact on the manpower, materiel and equipment, facilities, health services, and funding resource areas. It may also affect the environmental, transportation, industrial base, communications, and legal areas. It is not expected to have any measurable influence on HNS, although the training of allied military personnel, along with security assistance and other agreements, could affect the training base capacity.

SECTION J. HEALTH SERVICES

24. General

Theater, US, and aeromedical evacuation (AE) support are expanded to serve the mobilized force and provide the capability to treat, evacuate, receive, and redistribute casualties in the US. **Health services requirements are determined from decisions establishing the theater health services, intertheater and intratheater patient movement, and force health protection policies.** Several factors, such as casualty rates, population at risk, availability and readiness of health services units, transportation resources, blood supplies, and HNS assist in determining the theater health services required. **CONUS hospital beds and facilities are increased** to accommodate the expected flow of casualties and increases in the population of the CONUS support base. **The AE system is responsive in order** to employ the necessary contingency AE elements required to support the increased intratheater, intertheater, and CONUS evacuee requirements. **The nonactive duty beneficiary population eligible for government health care may be transferred to a managed care/TRICARE contract** as requirements for serving uniformed military beneficiaries approach the available capacity. **Military Department mobilization plans should include provisions for activating RC medical professionals for theater health services as required.**

25. Sources of Emergency Health Services

The sources of skilled health services manpower and hospital beds to meet emergency and wartime requirements for health care are listed in Figure IV-8, together with the options and actions required to mobilize additional health care capacity.

HEALTH SERVICES MOBILIZATION: SOURCES AND OPTIONS			
SITUATION	SOURCES OF HEALTH SERVICES	MOBILIZATION HEALTH SERIVCES	ACTIONS REQUIRED
Any level of emergency	Reserve Component (RC) health services units and individuals	Mobilize/activate volunteer individuals and units of the Selected Reserve	Military Departments order units and volunteer individuals to active duty within the limits of Presidential authorities invoked.
	Department of Veterans Affairs hospitals	Implement Department of Veterans Affairs Department of Defense (DOD) Contingency plan	DOD and Department of Veterans Affairs act in accordance with the Department of Veterans Affairs and DOD Health Resources Sharing and Emergency Operations Act (Public Law 97-174, as amended) when DOD requirements exceed supply of continental United States military hospitals.
	Host-nation health care systems	Activate host-nation support agreements	Geographic combatant commander requests support in accordance with agreements.
National emergency or war	RC health services units and individuals	Mobilize remaining RC health services units and individuals	Military Departments order RC units and individuals to active duty.
	Domestic civilian health care system	Transfer United States Public Health Service commissioned members to DOD or United States Coast Guard (USCG)	United States Public Health Service assigns members not already assigned under existing memorandums of understanding, to DOD or USCG with Secretary of Defense (SecDef) or Secretary of the Department of Homeland Security request and Presidential executive order.
		Activate National Disaster Medical System	SecDef acts under provisions of Public Health Service Act when bed requirements exceed capacity of DOD and Department of Veterans Affairs.

Figure IV-8. Health Services Mobilization: Sources and Options

26. Options for Mobilizing Health Services

a. **Options for mobilizing additional health and medical services professionals parallel those for other manpower skills.** In time of national emergency, the transfer of members of the United States Public Health Service (USPHS) commissioned corps to DOD may also provide additional health service professionals.

b. **Theater health services and aeromedical support is expanded** by calling up, transferring, and reassigning health and medical professionals, AC and RC health services units, and hospital ships deployed to the theater. See JP 4-02, *Health Services,* for specific information on organic DOD health services capabilities. Some mobilized RC personnel are assigned to CONUS's medical treatment facility as backfill. This enables the facilities to support care of returning casualties and the National Disaster Medical System (NDMS) missions.

c. **The CONUS health services base is expanded, as necessary, to provide care for casualties returned from the theater.** In addition to expanding CONUS military hospitals, this process may also include implementing, in turn, the Department of Veterans Affairs (DVA)-DOD Contingency Hospital System and the NDMS, which provide additional beds and professional staff from DVA and commercial civilian resources.

27. Impact of Health Services Mobilization on Other Resource Areas

The process of expanding theater health services may significantly burden the manpower, materiel and equipment, transportation, facilities, industrial base, training base, HNS, and legal resource areas. Increasing the CONUS health services base may significantly influence the manpower, materiel and equipment, facilities, and industrial base resource areas. It could also affect the transportation and training base areas, and it may require expanded legal authority. The transfer of dependent and retiree health care support to the managed care/TRICARE contract may have a significant impact on funding. The impact of mobilization in the remaining resource areas is not expected to be significant.

SECTION K. COMMUNICATIONS

28. Sources and Options for Mobilization Communications Support

Although the US military utilizes its own communications systems to execute many national defense/crisis response requirements, it frequently relies upon commercial providers to fulfill its administrative support needs. For this reason, **the Communications Act of 1934 provides the President with substantial authority during times of national emergency or war** to regulate and control virtually every form of telecommunications resource at the national and local levels. Included within this authority are devices and stations for wire, radio, and microwave transmissions. The Department of Homeland Security, the manager of the **NCS,** monitors situations that could develop into emergencies, provides recommendations for the use of resources, and maintains liaison with commercial providers. In time of national emergency or war, the President may invoke special war powers under the Communications Act (Title 47, USC, Section 606). These powers **allow the President to take immediate measures to ensure the continuous operation and security of telecommunications services** without negotiations or the consent of those who are affected. The Department of Defense's information networks support DOD and the Armed Forces. Other NCS assets support other departments and agencies of the USG. These other assets may be made available to DOD in crises and war when needed. The JS controls only a few communications assets, which are allocated during emergencies to provide additional communications in the theater.

29. Impact of Communications Mobilization Activities on Other Resource Areas

Virtually all communications resources required come from unused and redirected capacity maintained in peacetime. Some increases in personnel to accommodate additional operations, maintenance, and security needs may be required. The impact on other resource areas is expected to be minimal, except as the result of unexpected attrition or protracted operation that would generate requirements to replace fixed infrastructure.

SECTION L. HOST-NATION SUPPORT

30. Sources of Host-Nation Support

Manpower, equipment, facilities, and services provided by host or allied nations during war or emergency can offset requirements for corresponding US military resources that are not affordable or practical to maintain in peacetime. **A number of agreements are maintained with an ever-growing array of allies for defense cooperation.** Every effort should be made through the Department of State and DOD to establish some form of **mutual support**, **defense cooperation**, and/or **acquisition and cross-servicing agreements (ACSAs)** with US allies and friends around the globe. Initial cooperation can be achieved by helping to **establish a database of military and commercial capabilities available in each nation,** as well as standardized procedures to allow for rapid communication and understanding in a crisis situation. Additionally, this process enhances diplomatic efforts during peacetime and facilitates crisis management/contingency decision making by quickly providing more options to US and multinational leadership. **Direct HNS can be provided by an ally's military units that are organized and equipped for that specific purpose.** Financial arrangements may have already been established on a bilateral basis with a formula spelled out formally in a defense cooperation agreement. However, other arrangements may be made based on the situation at hand, to include multinational agreements with a regional or coalition organization or the United Nations (UN). Financial reimbursement policies and procedures may be developed through the use of in and out audit surveys (UN system) or some other process. Indirect support may be provided by host-nation commercial entities with licensing agreements or permissions granted by an allied government.

31. Coordinating Host-Nation Support

a. **Implement Existing Agreements.** Mutual support agreements, ACSAs, or defense cooperation agreements may be in effect between the US and the host nation. Such international agreements may adequately provide for support.

b. **Develop New Agreements.** The variable and uncertain nature of global security threats may create situations where it is necessary to negotiate new agreements providing for HNS. Commanders and persons responsible for mobilization should identify such needs as early as possible and consult with staff legal counsel to determine whether new agreements are required. Legal counsel should assist in the development of new agreements by coordinating with relevant CCMD staff judge advocates and by ensuring compliance with DOD and CJCS policy related to the negotiation of international agreements. The variable and uncertain nature of global security threats may create unforeseen situations where it may be necessary to seek ad hoc HNS. Such support is normally obtained through government-to-government negotiations or through negotiations conducted at a mutually agreed lower level.

See JP 4-08, Logistics in Support of Multinational Operations, *for more details.*

For North Atlantic Treaty Organization (NATO) doctrine, ratified by the US, see the Allied Joint Publication-4 Series of publications and associated NATO standardization agreements.

32. Impact of Mobilizing Host-Nation Support on Other Resource Areas

Implementation of existing or additional mutual support or defense cooperation agreements, depending on the nature of the support provided, **will affect the providing nation's or nations' resource areas,** particularly manpower, materiel and equipment, transportation assets, and possibly facilities. Careful consideration should be given to the impact upon the host nation and its capabilities compared to the offset of US resource requirements.

Intentionally Blank

CHAPTER V
MOBILIZATION PLANNING AND EXECUTION

> *"The Greeks by their laws, and the Romans by the spirit of their people, took care to put into the hands of their rulers no such engine of oppression as a standing army. Their system was to make every man a soldier, and oblige him to repair to the standard of his country whenever that was reared. This made them invincible; and the same remedy will make us so."*
>
> **Thomas Jefferson**
> **(Letter to Thomas Cooper, 1814)**

1. Introduction

a. **Mobilization plans** support CCDRs' OPLANs, concept plans, OPORDs, and campaign plans. They are detailed plans prepared by the Military Departments and DOD agencies. They are **based on policy and planning guidance** in the GEF, Defense Planning Guidance (DPG), GFMIG, DOD MMG, and in tasks specified by the CJCS in the JSCP. They **reflect requirements for force expansion** with RC units and IAs and for expansion of the CONUS base to sustain the mobilized force for as long as necessary to achieve military and national security objectives. Mobilization plans explain how force and resource expansion is to be accomplished.

b. Mobilization is a complex, time-sensitive process with many participants and activities. **Mobilization plans must be carefully integrated** among participants and the twelve resource areas. **Mobilization execution must be sequenced and carefully synchronized** to ensure that resources are available to the supported and supporting commanders when needed. **The CJCS,** supported by the JS, **integrates mobilization planning** and monitors the status and progress of mobilization execution. **CJCS advises SecDef** on establishing priorities; allocating resource shortages among claimants; and redirecting execution activities, when necessary, to eliminate bottlenecks and overcome unforeseen problems. The collection of lessons learned information throughout the mobilization process is a vital component of the planning process. Lessons learned, when properly applied, will enhance joint capabilities, advance force readiness, and assist in the planning of future mobilizations.

c. The Mobilization Information Management Plan (MIMP) provides guidance on information systems related to mobilization planning and execution. This plan identifies the flow of information related to mobilization under both deliberate planning and CAP, and is designed to provide a coherent and accurate status of mobilization efforts. Appendix C, "Mobilization Information Management Plan," contains specific policies regarding the MIMP.

d. Opportunities to determine the validity of mobilization plans and practice mobilization procedures are provided by periodic **CJCS-sponsored worldwide command post exercises.** These exercises may involve SecDef, OSD, the JS, the Services, the CCMDs, and other selected USG departments and agencies. These may be augmented by field training exercises conducted by CCMDs and/or Services.

e. **This chapter provides a joint perspective of mobilization planning, execution, and reporting.** It explains the relationships between mobilization plans, OPLANs, and campaign plans. It introduces the mobilization estimate of the situation, a tool to assist the thought processes of commanders and mobilization planners. It describes the joint mobilization planning processes. It also provides an overview of the mobilization execution process.

SECTION A. MOBILIZATION PLANNING

2. Mobilization Planning and Operation Plans

a. The GEF, DPG, and DOD Master Mobilization Plan provide SecDef guidance for mobilization planning in support of joint operations. The CJCS amplifies the guidance in the JSCP.

b. CJCSI 3110.13, *Mobilization Guidance for the Joint Strategic Capabilities Plan (U)*, guides the Military Departments and CCDRs in preparing mobilization plans that support the CCDRs' contingency plans. The planning guidance is focused on the areas of manpower and industrial mobilization. Manpower mobilization requirements derived for each contingency establish the level of mobilization assumed for each contingency and drive the determination of mobilization requirements in the twelve resource areas. The industrial mobilization guidance requires the Military Departments to conduct industrial preparedness planning and to maintain a production base that will support contingency requirements.

c. During JOPP, **the Military Departments furnish mobilization-related information to the CCDRs,** who incorporate it into the OPLANs under development or revision. The major mobilization plans and planning systems are shown in Figure V-1.

d. **Manpower mobilization information** furnished by the Military Departments for inclusion in OPLANs **provides the foundation for detailed planning** in the other resource areas. This information comprises the number of AC and RC personnel required by Service and skill for each option included in the OPLAN. **The functions are:**

(1) **Direct support for each option** (i.e., units and individuals needed to augment the supported commander's combat and support force).

Major Mobilization Plans and Planning Systems

- Adaptive Planning and Execution System
- Army Mobilization Operations Planning and Execution System
- Navy Capabilities and Mobilization Plan
- Air Force War and Mobilization Plan
- Marine Corps Mobilization, Activation, Integration, and Deactivation Plan
- Coast Guard Manpower Mobilization and Support Plan

Figure V-1. Major Mobilization Plans and Planning Systems

---

(2) **CONUS base** (i.e., units and individuals required for the level of CONUS-based expansion to support each option).

(3) **CONUS and outside the continental United States (OCONUS) backfill** (i.e., units and individuals required to replace those deployed to the theater).

(4) **Strategic transportation** (i.e., units and individuals needed to augment peacetime strategic air mobility and sealift capabilities).

3. Mobilization Plans and Military Campaign Plans

A campaign plan has important implications for mobilization planners. Firm strategic objectives, force levels, and time constraints are key elements of information with which the commander and mobilization planner can **execute mobilization planning** and **initiate additional force and resource expansion options** if needed. Additional industrial mobilization and the reinstitution of the draft may be indicated in the campaign plan if there is an expectation of a long war with high materiel and personnel attrition. Conversely, if the campaign plan expects a short war with low attrition, mobilization planners can concentrate on managing mobilization at a lower level.

A more complete discussion of campaign plans is provided in JP 5-0, Joint Operation Planning.

4. Mobilization Estimate of the Situation

a. **A commander's estimate of the situation** provides a logical process of reasoning by which **a commander considers all the circumstances affecting the military situation and arrives at a decision as to a COA to be taken to accomplish the mission.** A staff estimate is similar, with the major difference being that the culmination of the staff estimate process is a conclusion or recommendation communicated to the commander.

b. The mobilization estimate format in Appendix E, "Mobilization Estimate," applies the staff estimate concept to mobilization planning. **The mobilization estimate provides a tool for mobilization planners to make a systematic appraisal of mobilization requirements and options.** Although designed from the point of view of the JS J-4, the format may be adapted to fit the circumstances for other JS directorates and of mobilization planners on the CCDR, Service component commander, and Service headquarters staffs.

c. The mobilization estimate requires input from all functional areas of the JS, Service staffs, and the corresponding staff sections at the CCMDs. Although not every situation demands an extensive planning effort, **the mobilization process is complex and involves interactions that may influence the outcome of the analysis.** It is important, therefore, that the mobilization proponent on a staff establishes and maintains effective communications with the other staff sections.

d. **The accuracy of the information gathered** to complete paragraph 2 of the estimate and the quality of the analysis made in paragraph 3 of the estimate **are essential to the validity of the mobilization estimate.**

(1) **In paragraph 2, a net assessment is made of the mobilization capability in each resource area.** The net assessment consists of the time-phased mobilization capability or capacity in each resource area compared to the requirements of each COA. Shortages or overages should be identified and quantified in terms of the unit of measure used in the area (e.g., number of personnel, training seats, short tons, hospital beds, days of supply).

(2) **In paragraph 3, estimates of the impacts of mobilization activities in each resource area on the other areas are made** to determine if the mobilization action is feasible. For example, when a COA requires training base expansion, the analysis process for paragraph 3 should establish that there are enough qualified instructors, facilities, equipment, and medical support for an expanded training establishment. A shortage in one or more of these areas will limit the training base expansion and may render the COA infeasible.

e. **The completed analysis should support conclusions concerning the feasibility or infeasibility of each COA** with respect to mobilization and the ultimate staff recommendation on the best COA.

5. Mobilization Planning During Deliberate Planning

During peacetime, mobilization planners in the JPEC participate in two primary activities: maintaining a mobilization base and participating in JOPP to develop detailed mobilization plans to support OPLANs.

a. **Maintaining a mobilization base** at resource levels adequate to support the mobilization requirements of OPLANs **is a full-time peacetime task** for mobilization planners in all resource areas. Training exercises are used to evaluate adequacy of mobilization plans, resources, and training. **The mobilization base is defined as the total of all resources available, or that can be made available, to meet foreseeable wartime needs.** The two most critical resources in the mobilization base are manpower and industrial base capacity because of the time and expense involved in developing skilled military and civilian personnel and technologically sophisticated military equipment.

(1) **Manpower Programs.** With policy and planning guidance provided by OSD, **the Military Departments manage manpower programs,** which include RC manpower pools, with the numbers of personnel and the skill mix required to meet estimated wartime sustainability requirements. The IRR and other IA pools are maintained by a combination of laws and policies, such as the 8-year military service obligation (Title 10, USC, Section 12103) and programs for recruiting and retaining skilled RC personnel. Manpower programs are funded through the PPBE process. Manpower mobilization base maintenance is also supported by the SSS, which will draw on a pool of 18- to 26-year-old registrants if a military draft is required to sustain the force and is enabled by legislation.

(2) **Industrial Preparedness Programs.** Military Department and DOD agency **objectives for materiel and equipment sustainability are to maintain war reserve stocks of critical equipment** in sufficient quantities to fulfill estimated sustainability requirements until industrial base output can be expanded to meet expected consumption rates. **The basis for industrial preparedness planning is the CCDRs' CIL.** The CIL is the accumulation of current inventory items (consumable and non-consumable) that each CCDR has identified as deficient through routine reporting in the CJCS's Joint Forces Readiness Report.

(3) **Maintaining a mobilization base in the other resource areas requires planning and investment** by the Military Departments for mobilization activities such as facilities and training base expansion, mobilization of strategic and CONUS transportation resources, and expanding health services capabilities.

b. **Deliberate planning** occurs in non-crisis situations. Mobilization planning takes place in every phase of JOPP. In deliberate planning, the total requirement for RC forces to support the OPLAN must be identified and documented once the plan is complete. The RC requirements summary tables list the aggregate RC support necessary for the execution of the OPLAN, and are used as the numerical justification for requesting specific legal authorities and levels of mobilization, and will be included in annex A (Task Organization). **Chairman of the Joint Chiefs of Staff Manual (CJCSM) 3130.03,** *Adaptive Planning and Execution (APEX) Planning Formats and Guidance,* **establishes the standard formats and guidance for developing** OPLANs.

For further information, see CJCSI 3110.13, Mobilization Guidance for the Joint Strategic Capabilities Plan.

c. **Functions of the APEX System.** The APEX functions include strategic guidance, concept development, plan development, and plan refinement (see Figure V-2). Each step of the RC requirements process (in context with the APEX functions) is described in subsequent subparagraphs.

(1) **Strategic Guidance.** The GFMIG provides for the apportionment of major combat forces and selected special operations forces (SOF). These and other force requirements are broadly defined by the supported CCDR's strategic concept and **time-phased force and deployment data (TPFDD)** letter of instruction (LOI) to guide plan development. Strategic guidance should:

(a) **Consider implications of RC use** that are not limited to the strategic guidance function. Apportioned RC combat forces and major theater combat service/combat service support (CSS) are known but visibility of smaller RC units will only occur after sourcing is complete. Provide input or feedback on RC requirements and assumptions to the staffing of high-level guidance documents such as the GEF, DPG, JSCP, and CJCSI 3110.13, *Mobilization Guidance for the Joint Strategic Capabilities Plan.*

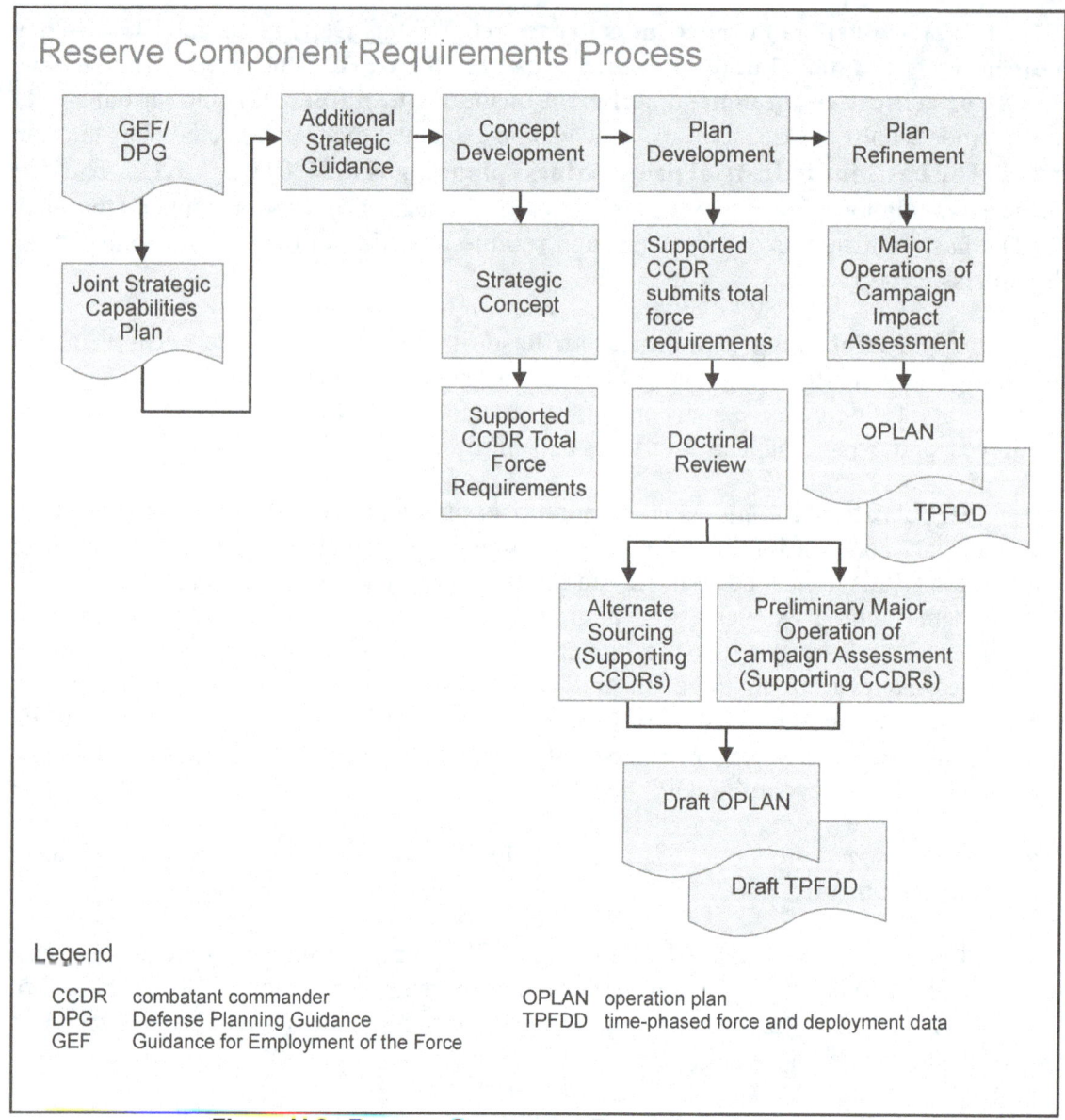

Figure V-2. Reserve Component Requirements Process

(b) **Facilitate the planner's development** of the supported CCDR's TPFDD LOI and related actions to ensure that RC mobilization guidance and taskings are visible and understood for apportioned RC major combat forces, SOF units, and theater level combat support and CSS units.

(c) **Facilitate the review of the LOI** to ensure the stated requirement for the aggregate RC requirements are contained in annex A (Task Organization) to the OPLAN.

(2) **Concept Development.** During this function, the mobilization planner becomes familiar with the CCDR's strategic concept and TPFDD LOI and checks each for consistent RC planning factors such as force structure available during the planning cycle, scheduled conversions, activations, and inactivations. If there are inconsistencies, the

mobilization planner provides immediate feedback to the supported CCDR. The product created during concept development is the supported CCDR's total joint force requirement.

      (3) **Plan Development.** During plan development, plan TPFDD sourcing occurs (see Figure V-2). The Services select units to meet the time-phased requirements of the supported CCDR. When the Services source a plan TPFDD, the planner, with the mobilization planner's advice, adds an important dimension to the sourcing process by considering where Service capabilities reside. These selected units may be active forces, a combination of AC and RC, or even combinations that include civilian and contractor support. After requirements are determined, there must be a concerted effort to identify component sourcing, either AC or RC, to increase the accuracy of specifying the total RC units and manpower required. At the end of this phase, the draft TPFDD is available. Normally, this provides the bulk of the RC requirement and enables the supported CCMD's mobilization planner to create the draft RC requirements. At this point, the TPFDD is sourced and considered final. However, the RC requirements must still be finalized by each Service using TPFDD data. The Services and supporting CCDRs give the supported CCDR draft data that must be compiled and included in the supporting plans to complete the RC requirement (see Figure V-3). Once a plan is completed, the original mobilization assumptions are either validated or refuted.

      (4) **Plan Refinement.** In plan refinement, the CCDR, in coordination with the JPEC, conducts a formal review of the plan. The JS J-4 mobilization planner and other JS directorates review the RC requirements summaries and supporting data. The supporting CCDRs and Services finalize requirements in several areas: movement of the force, mobilization and deployment support, sustainment operations, and backfill capabilities. CONUS-based and other forces supporting the deployment are not included on the TPFDD, but the requirements are identified and planned. During execution planning each requirement is justified, the RC unit is selected and called to active duty.

    d. **RC Requirements Summary Tables.** The summary tables identify RC forces and

---

Operational Plan Reserve Component Requirements

- Reserve Components in the Area of Responsibility
  - Supported combatant commander (CCDR) obtains from time-phased force and deployment data after Services source force list
- Transportation Enablers
  - Supported CCDR obtains from US Transportation Command
- Mobilization/Deployment Supporters
  - Supported CCDR obtains from Services
- Active Component Backfill
  - Supported CCDR obtains from Services

Figure V-3. Operation Plan Reserve Component Requirements

---

support forces required to accomplish the following: deploy to the GCC's area of responsibility (AOR); move the force; assist in mobilization, deployment, and sustainment; and backfill departing AC units and individuals. Too often, planners are unaware of the total RC requirement to support the OPLAN under development. CJCSM 3130.03, *Adaptive Planning and Execution (APEX) Planning Formats and Guidance,* JSCP; and CJCSI 3110.13, *Mobilization Guidance for the Joint Strategic Capabilities Plan,* require completion of annex A (Task Organization) to OPLANs. The RC portion of annex A (Task Organization) should contain the number of RC requirement summaries necessary to support requests for mobilization legal authorities. For instance, if flexible deterrent options (FDOs) within phase 0 (Shape) or phase I (Deter) of the plan require PRC and a subsequent phase requires partial mobilization, separate RC requirements summaries must be prepared for each of these phases to support the requests for PRC and subsequently for partial mobilization. It is not necessary to prepare a separate RC requirement summary for each OPLAN FDO. Mobilization planners analyze FDOs in the aggregate to determine the point at which PRC becomes necessary and prepare one summary to support the request. These summaries provide senior leadership with the data required to determine the level of mobilization necessary to execute various functions during planning. Figure V-4 is an example of a CCDR's RC requirements summary to support an FDO associated with an OPLAN. This summary would be used by the mobilization planner to justify a recommendation to request a PRC.

EXAMPLE: RESERVE COMPONENT REQUIREMENTS SUMMARY							
OPERATION PLAN 1234	X	FLEXIBLE DETERRENT OPTION(s) RC26			PLAN EXECUTION		
Service	RC in Area of Responsibility	Move the Force	Assist Mobilization/ Deploy/Sustain		Backfill		Total RC Personnel by Service
			Individual Mobilization Augmentee	Individual Ready Reserve/Selective Reserve	Continental US	Outside Continental US	
US Army	0	1,200	310	900	700	350	3,460
US Navy	0	300	33	1,200	600	220	2,353
US Air Force	0	1,300	140	1,550	990	20	4,000
US Marine Corps	0	25	60	90	270	150	595
US Coast Guard	0	0	3	15	0	10	28
TOTALS		2,825	546	3,755	2,560	750	10,436
Legend							
RC Reserve Component							

Figure V-4. Example: Reserve Component Requirements Summary

(1) **RC in AOR.** During the plan development (following CCDR submission of total joint force requirements and development of a draft TPFDD), the Services calculate and provide the supported CCDR with two sets of data (RC unit and RC non-unit personnel in the TPFDD) that produce the RC manpower numbers in the "RC in AOR" column. This number is calculated to provide the best estimate of the RC portion of TPFDD non-unit personnel. This includes planned fillers and replacements, who may not all come from the

AC, particularly if planning the second of two major operations or campaigns. For example, if 10,000 fillers and replacements are planned for deploying units, a planner might estimate that 2,000 of these would be RC. This could be based on predetermined assumptions such as physical location of active or RC forces; time to call-up and deploy RC forces; duration of decisive force in plan execution; or requirements to consider another major operation or campaign. Even though the plan and the TPFDD may not specify AC or RC for fillers and replacements, the mobilization planner provides the planner with assistance to define the RC portion of this requirement to complete the table.

(2) **Move the Force, Assist Mobilization, Deployment, or Sustainment, and Backfill.** During plan refinement, the Services, supporting CCDRs, USTRANSCOM, and other agencies define their non-TPFDD requirements to support complete plan execution. The Services coordinate with these organizations to identify actual RC forces needed to meet these requirements.

6. **Crisis Action Planning**

a. A crisis is an incident or situation that typically develops rapidly and creates a condition of such diplomatic, economic, or military importance that the President or SecDef considers a commitment of US military forces and resources to achieve national objectives. It may occur with little or no warning, develop rapidly, and require accelerated decision making. Sometimes a single crisis may spawn another crisis elsewhere.

b. CAP provides the CJCS and CCDRs a process for getting vital decision-making information up the chain of command to the President and SecDef. CAP facilitates information sharing among the members of the JPEC and the integration of military advice from the CJCS in the analysis of military options. Additionally, CAP allows the President and SecDef to communicate their decisions rapidly and accurately through the CJCS to the CCDRs, subordinate and supporting commanders, Services, and CSAs to initiate detailed military planning, change deployment posture of the identified force, and execute military options. It also outlines the mechanisms for monitoring the execution of the operation.

c. CAP encompasses the activities associated with the time-sensitive development of OPORDs for the deployment, employment, and sustainment of assigned, attached, and allocated forces and capabilities in response to a situation that may result in actual military operations. While deliberate planning normally is conducted in anticipation of future events, CAP is based on circumstances that exist at the time planning occurs. CAP can use plans developed in deliberate planning for a similar contingency. If unanticipated circumstances occur, and no plan proves adequate for the operational circumstances, then CAP and execution would begin mission analysis under JOPP in a "no plan" situation. There are always situations arising in the present that might require US military response. Such situations may approximate those previously planned for in deliberate planning, although it is unlikely they would be identical, and sometimes they will be completely unanticipated. The time available to plan responses to such real-time events is short. In as little as a few days, commanders and staffs must develop and approve a feasible COA with TPFDD; publish the plan or order; prepare forces; ensure sufficient communications systems support; and arrange sustainment for the employment of US military forces. Figure V-5 provides a comparison of deliberate planning and CAP.

DELIBERATE PLANNING AND CRISIS ACTION PLANNING COMPARISON		
	Deliberate Planning	Crisis Action Planning
Time available	As defined in authoritative directives (normally 6+ months)	Situation dependent (hours, days, up to 12 months)
Environment	Distributed, collaborative planning	Distributed, collaborative planning and execution
JPEC involvement	Full JPEC participation may be limited for security reasons.	Full JPEC participation may be limited for security reasons.
APEX operational activities	Situational awareness Planning	Situational awareness Planning Execution
APEX functions	Strategic guidance Concept development Plan development Plan assessment	Strategic guidance Concept development Plan development Plan assessment
Document assigning planning task	CJCS issues: 1. JSCP 2. Planning directive 3. WARNORD (for short suspense planning)	CJCS issues: 1. WARNORD 2. PLANORD 3. SecDef-approved ALERTORD
Forces for planning	Apportioned in JSCP	Allocated in WARNORD, PLANORD, or ALERTORD
Planning guidance	CJCS issues JSCP or WARNORD CCDR issues planning directive and TPFDD LOI	CJCS issues WARNORD, PLANORD, or ALERTORD CCDR issues WARNORD, PLANORD, or ALERTORD and TPFDD LOI to subordinates, supporting commands, and supporting agencies
COA selection	CCDR selects COA and submits strategic concept to CJCS for review and SecDef approval	CCDR develops commander's estimate with recommended COA
Concept of operations approval	SecDef approves commander's strategic concept, disapproves or approves for further planning	President/SecDef approve COA, disapproves or approves further planning
Final planning product	Campaign plan Level 1–4 contingency plan	Operation order
Final planning product approval	CCDR submits final plan to CJCS for review and SecDef for approval	CCDR submits final plan to President/SecDef for approval
Execution document	Not applicable	CJCS issues SecDef-approved execution order CCDR issues execution order

Legend			
ALERTORD	alert order	JSCP	Joint Strategic Capabilities Plan
APEX	Adaptive Planning and Execution	LOI	letter of instruction
CCDR	combatant commander	PLANORD	planning order
CJCS	Chairman of the Joint Chiefs of Staff	SecDef	Secretary of Defense
COA	course of action	TPFDD	time-phased force and deployment data
JPEC	joint planning and execution community	WARNORD	warning order

Figure V-5. Deliberate Planning and Crisis Action Planning Comparison

d. In a crisis, situational awareness is continuously updated by the latest all-source intelligence and operations reports. An adequate and feasible military response in a crisis demands flexible procedures that consider time available, rapid and effective communications, and relevant previous planning products whenever possible.

e. **In a crisis or time-sensitive situation, the CCDR uses the initial CAP situational awareness phase to review previously prepared contingency plans for suitability.** The CCDR converts these plans to executable OPORDs or develops OPORDs from scratch when no useful contingency plan exists.

f. CAP activities are similar to deliberate planning activities, but CAP is based on dynamic, real-world conditions. CAP procedures provide for the rapid and effective exchange of information and analysis, the timely preparation of military COAs for consideration by the President or SecDef, and the prompt transmission of their decisions to the JPEC. CAP activities may be performed sequentially or in parallel, with supporting and subordinate plans or OPORDs being developed concurrently. The exact flow of activities is largely determined by the time available to complete the planning and by the significance of the crisis (see Figure V-5). The following paragraphs summarize the activities and interaction that occur during CAP. Refer to the CJCSM 3122 series and CJCSM 3130 series of publications, which address planning policies and procedures, for detailed procedures.

g. CAP activities emphasize the importance of lessons learned collection in the process of operation planning.

For further detailed discussion of the Joint Lessons Learned Information System (JLLIS), see CJCSI 3150.25, Joint Lessons Learned Program.

SECTION B. MOBILIZATION EXECUTION

7. Mobilization Decisions and Orders

a. **CJCS recommends to SecDef the assets that are to be called up and their planned use** when RC forces are to be mobilized to augment the AC. **SecDef approval is required for the execution of a mobilization OPORD.** Figure V-6 shows the mobilization execution planning process. In preparing a mobilization recommendation to the President, the following should be considered:

(1) Assessments of the Services, CCDRs, and Service component commanders.

(2) Input from the JS.

(3) Technical advice, legal opinions, and policy considerations from OSD.

b. **After the President's decision to initiate mobilization, SecDef directs the Military Departments to proceed.** The Services publish mobilization orders in accordance with their respective procedures. OSD may issue implementation instructions and provide additional policy guidance, if required.

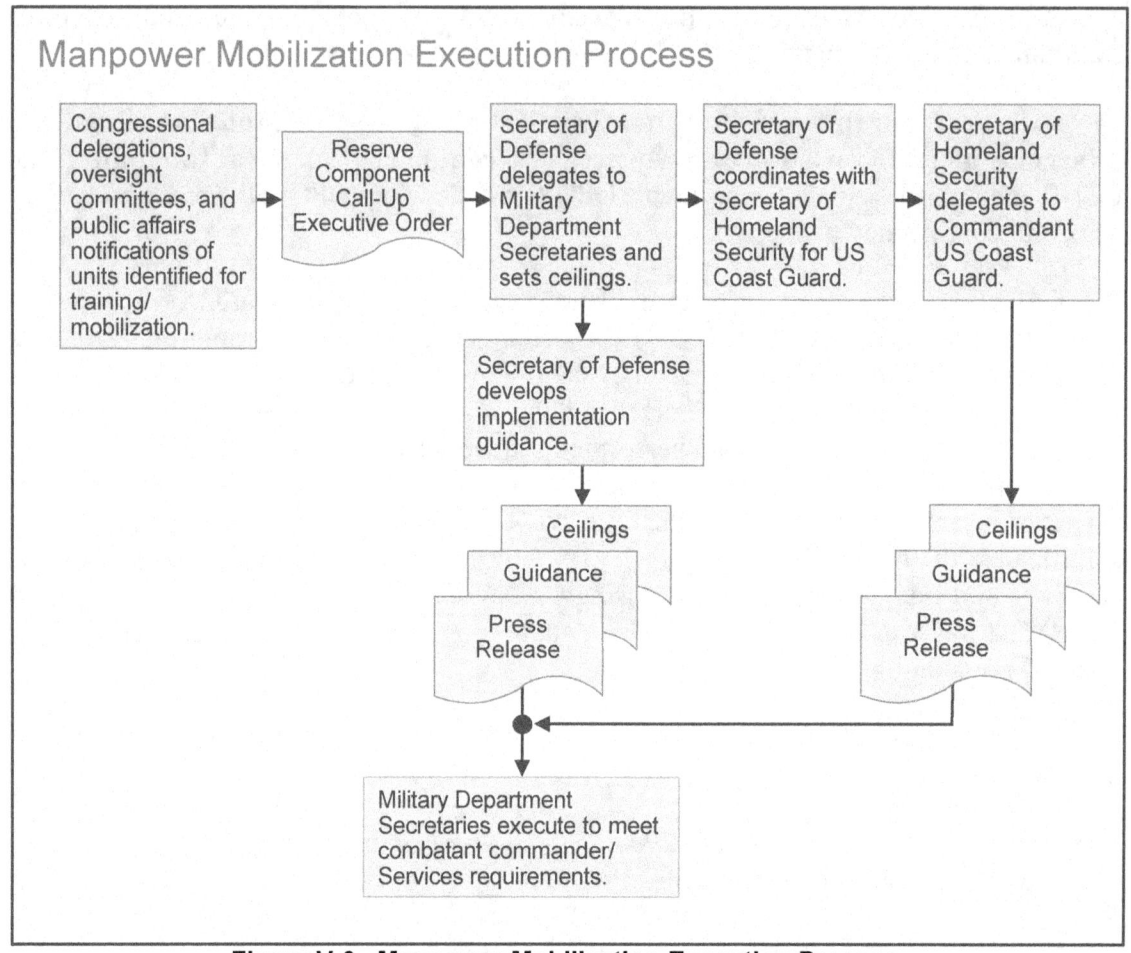

Figure V-6. Manpower Mobilization Execution Process

c. **Some mobilization actions require the President or SecDef to notify Congress.** For example, some legal authorities require reports at specific intervals. Others require specific information on how the authority is being used and how long it will be needed. Reports on expenditures related to the crisis are also required. The CJCS and the DOD Comptroller are normally responsible for preparing these reports, which require continuous coordination throughout the JPEC. Figure V-7 illustrates the RC decision-making process. DODI 1235.12, *Accessing the Reserve Components (RC),* provides detailed guidelines and procedures for the mobilization execution process and the required level of authorities and approval.

8. Monitoring the Status and Progress of Mobilization

Because mobilization involves interrelated activities in twelve resource areas, SecDef, OSD, CJCS, Secretaries of the Military Departments, and other members of the JPEC need accurate and timely information on the status and progress of mobilization. **Information received by proponents in each of the resource areas is analyzed and coordinated with the other resource area proponents** to provide decision makers with recommendations for controlling, replanning, redirecting, or stopping mobilization operations. CJCSM 3122.01A, *Joint Operation Planning and Execution System (JOPES), Volume I (Planning Policies and Procedures),* provides detailed procedures and automated information to support operations planning and execution.

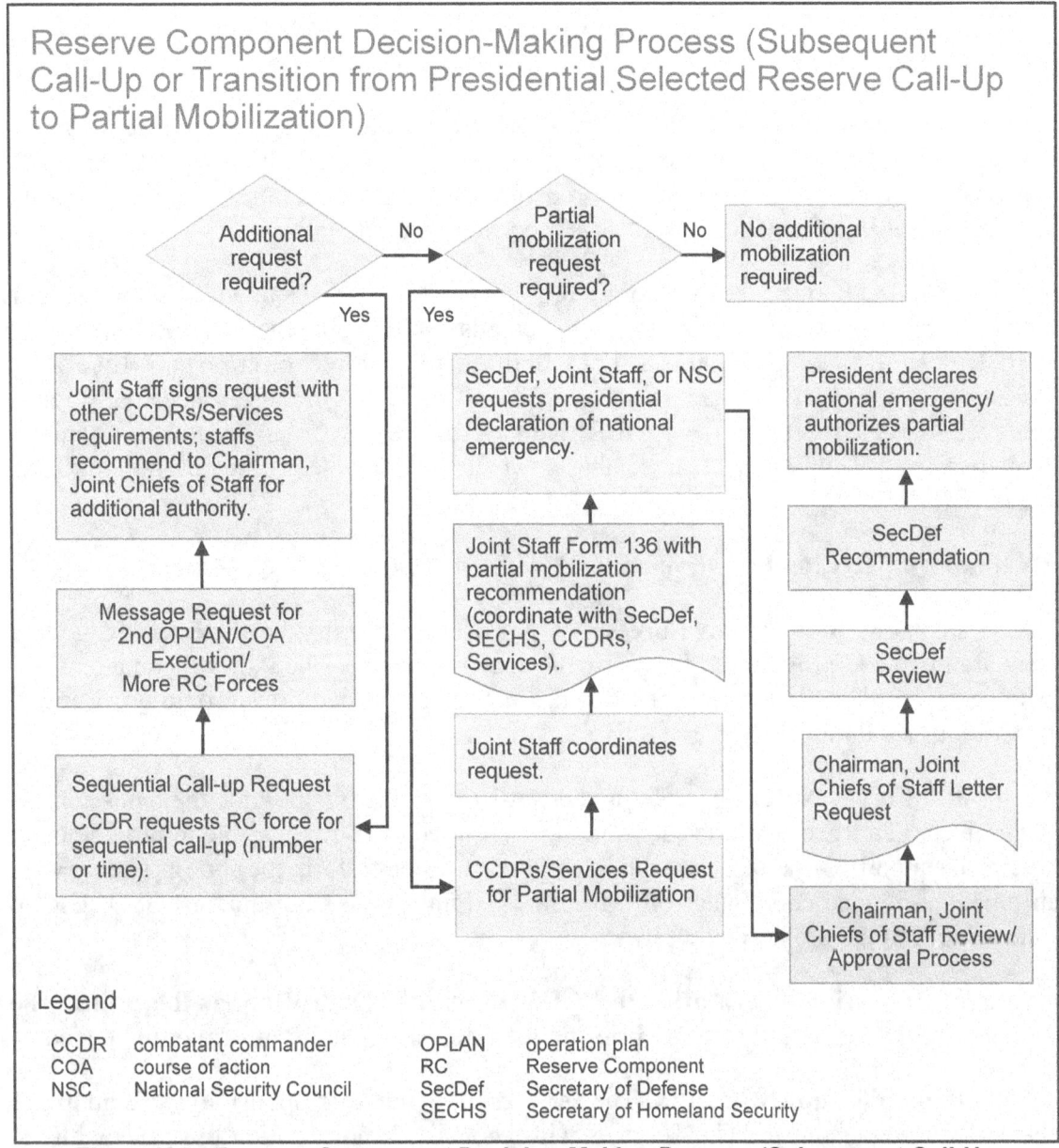

Figure V-7. Reserve Component Decision-Making Process (Subsequent Call-Up or Transition from Presidential Selected Reserve Call-Up to Partial Mobilization)

SECTION C. MOBILIZATION REPORTING

9. Reporting Requirements

a. Reporting involves extracting information obtained from monitoring activities, then providing the data to appropriate organizations involved with mobilization and demobilization. The mobilization planner responds to formal and informal reporting requirements. The formal requirements are those specified in statutes or directives such as reporting to Congress, the JS, or the Services. Three formal reports are generated: RC requirements from annex A (Task Organization) of each OPLAN which lists the total RC requirements; the mobilization report (MOBREP); and during partial mobilization, the President's report to Congress. Figure V-8 illustrates the information flow for these reports.

b. Congressional requests and queries may require informal or special case reporting. Future rotation plans, mobilization capability or status requests, limitations on reservists, seasonal or personal information, and redeployment and demobilization plans may be required to fulfill informal or special case reporting requirements.

c. Once the Services begin to order RC units and individuals to active duty, the joint reporting process begins. Joint reporting entails reporting on people and units. The MOBREP shows people available and/or mobilized. After direction from the Office of the Assistant Secretary of Defense, Reserve Affairs (OASD[RA]), the Services daily (or as otherwise directed) submit the MOBREP to OASD(RA). Units update the Status of Resources and Training System database, which is available for review on the local area network.

10. Four Subjects Require Reporting

a. **Problems in Providing Forces.** The Services must notify the requester and the JS if they are unable to provide RC forces by the specified dates. Then, the JS can attempt to resolve the problem. This is not a formal report, but is required promptly to ensure expeditious resolution.

b. **RC Forces No Longer Required.** All organizations monitor their missions to determine when RC capabilities are no longer required or if it is feasible to provide other means of support. Organizations with releasable RC forces inform the appropriate Service; in turn, the Service coordinates with the JS J-3 Joint Force Coordinator/USSOCOM to determine if forces are needed elsewhere.

c. **Mobilization Information to JS J-3 Director of Operations as Required.** The JS J-4 coordinates with the JS J-3 briefing team to ascertain the information needed.

d. **Demobilization Schedules.** The Services have primary responsibility to demobilize their units and personnel. The Services will reconcile demobilization timelines with the supported CCDR's priorities and will notify CCDRs who have assigned/attached RC forces of the planned demobilization dates and corresponding timeline accounting for demobilization movement and out processing.

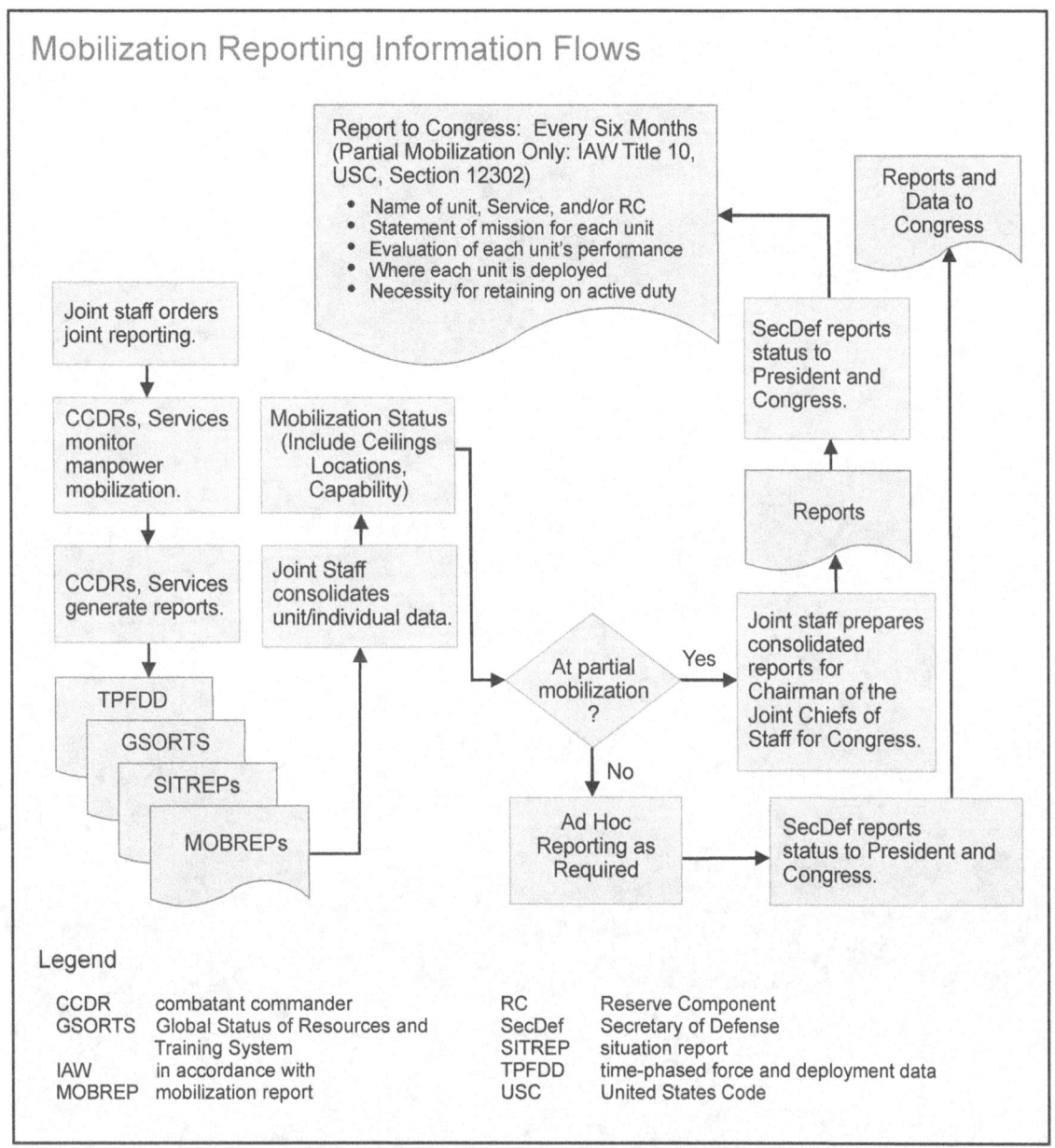

Figure V-8. Mobilization Reporting Information Flows

Intentionally Blank

CHAPTER VI
JOINT DEMOBILIZATION PLANNING AND EXECUTION

"Resolved, that the commanding officer be and he is hereby directed to discharge the troops now in the service of the United States, except twenty-five privates, to guard the stores at Fort Pitt, and fifty-five to guard the stores at West Point and other magazines, with a proportionate number of officers; no officer to remain in service above the rank of a captain."

Resolution of the Continental Congress
(Disbanding the Continental Army, 2 June 1784)

1. Introduction

a. **Demobilization is the process of transitioning from a conflict situation or from a wartime military establishment and defense-based civilian economy to a peacetime configuration** while maintaining national security and economic vitality. It involves more than releasing personnel from active duty, deactivating units, and reorganizing the RC. Although these activities drive the process, capability or capacity in the other resource areas must be reduced and reorganized at the same time. As in mobilization, **activities in each resource area during demobilization will affect each of the others.** For this reason, close coordination among resource area proponents is just as important during demobilization as it is during mobilization.

b. **This chapter provides the national and joint military perspectives of demobilization planning and execution.** It also provides guidelines for demobilization planning and execution and an overview of demobilization activities in the twelve resource areas.

2. Demobilization and National Security

a. From a national perspective, **the results of a successful demobilization process should put the US in a position to respond to future challenges to our national security.** Policies should be established to regulate the pace of demobilization and **retain the military capability required to ensure post-conflict national security commitments.** Force structure changes are not inherent to the demobilization process. **Industrial base and other civil sector resources mobilized during the conflict will be released** to fuel the post-conflict national economy.

b. **The scope of demobilization will vary according to the extent of the preceding mobilization.** The scope of mobilization can range from a relatively brief use of a few volunteer reservists to a protracted force and resource expansion well beyond the original peacetime levels.

c. From a joint military perspective, **demobilization plans should reflect the post-conflict missions of supported CCDRs** and be synchronized with plans for recovery, reconstitution, and redeployment operations. **DOD policies for the release of reservists and RC units ordered to active duty should first reflect military requirements** and then considerations of equity and fairness for military personnel and their families. The demobilization personnel management programs of the Military Departments will be challenged to facilitate the return of Service members and their families to civilian life and need to provide substantive **transition assistance,** such as screening for medical care requirements and potential long-term health care support, and assistance in availing themselves of statutory reemployment rights, as members reenter the civilian workforce. Title 10, USC, Section 1144(c) mandates participation of all Service members in the Transition Assistance Program of DOD. These requirements must be completed prior to release from active duty at the demobilization location of the Service component. National Guard and reserve units and members ordered to active duty to augment the AC will, consistent with operational requirements, receive priority for redeployment. They will be released from active duty as expeditiously as possible and will remain eligible for transition services up to 180 days after release from active duty.

3. Demobilization Planning Guidelines

Studies of the demobilizations following the two World Wars and the Gulf War provide valuable lessons for today's demobilization planners and have been distilled into the following **guidelines illustrated in Figure VI-1 for demobilization planning and execution:**

a. **Mission First.** Demobilization plans must support the post-conflict mission as it evolves. **The supported commander's immediate postwar priorities should come first.** As the transition to a post-conflict state proceeds, long-range national security objectives should drive demobilization activities to ensure the Armed Forces are prepared for the next crisis.

b. **Begin Planning Early.** Demobilization planning should begin soon after mobilization starts.

c. **Coordinate and Communicate Plans and Policies.** The demobilization policies and procedures that worked best in the past were those that had been developed and coordinated by interested personnel and agencies both within and outside DOD. Public information programs that explained demobilization policies helped gain and maintain public support.

Demobilization Planning Guidelines

- Mission first.
- Begin planning early.
- Coordinate and communicate plans and policies.

Figure VI-1. Demobilization Planning Guidelines

SECTION A. DEMOBILIZATION PLANNING

4. Planning Considerations

a. **Demobilizing the Armed Forces** could be a relatively straightforward return of mobilized/activated units and individuals to their former status. It could also be a broader process including measures such as deactivation of units, rapid discharge of individuals, and a major reorganization of the RC. Similarly, **demobilization of the defense industry** could range from an almost total reconversion of a defense-oriented industrial base to a simple reduction in the output of a few providers who surged production to meet the near-term demands of a short-lived crisis.

b. **Recovery activities must also be planned along with demobilization.** These include activities for restoring force readiness (reset/reconstitution) and controlling the rate of industrial base conversion to avoid disrupting the national economy. As manpower is being released from the Services and industrial production is being cut back, the Services must retain or replace skilled manpower required to restore readiness and replenish war reserves and other stocks to be prepared for the next crisis.

c. **Demobilization planning is accomplished at two levels.** At the national level, the President and SecDef must decide on the rate of demobilization and the size and composition of the post-conflict force structure and its resource base. These **national-level** decisions drive demobilization planning and resource requests at the **theater and supporting levels.** They also guide the post-conflict activities of the supported and supporting commanders.

d. **The supported CCDR remains the key to military demobilization.** The supported GCC's mission and requirements should take precedence over all others. **Other general planning factors should include:**

(1) The situation and requirements in other theaters. SecDef, with the advice of CJCS, should establish a priority of support.

(2) Future missions in the theater.

(3) Availability of strategic lift for redeployment.

(4) CONUS reception and processing capacities for manpower and materiel.

(5) Lessons learned from previous demobilization operations.

5. Recovery Planning

a. **Recovery planning should be closely coordinated with demobilization planning.** Recovery includes the reset actions necessary in the theater and CONUS base to restore force readiness and a credible capability to respond, in the short term, to a future threat. **Included activities are to:**

(1) Rebuild major equipment items.

(2) Restore personnel strength and training readiness to required wartime levels for future contingencies.

(3) Restore war reserve stocks to acceptable levels.

(4) Maintain essential industrial surge and expansion capabilities.

(5) Finalize recovery of redeployed equipment returned to CONUS or address shortages created by remain-behind equipment requirements.

(6) Terminate war-related contracts for the convenience of the government.

(7) Reestablish contracts at garrison or home base as troops return.

(8) Restore pre-positioning ships and embarked equipment and stores.

b. **The planning and resourcing of these activities are the responsibility of OSD and the Military Departments.** CJCS assists SecDef in providing strategic direction for these efforts.

SECTION B. EXECUTION

6. General

Demobilization activities can begin before the end of the crisis or war as the need for resources diminishes and assets for demobilization support become available. **Most demobilization actions will commence following the conflict** when immediate post-conflict missions have been assigned by the supported CCDR and requirements for military forces and resources decline. Although demobilization, like mobilization, is essentially a Military Department responsibility, **the supported and supporting commanders play coordinating and synchronizing roles.** In any event, **the CCDRs monitor the status and progress of demobilization and concurrent recovery operations** to assess the adequacy of actions to restore readiness of assigned forces to required levels for future conflicts.

7. Demobilization Execution

Following redeployment, the Military Departments deactivate units or return them to a reserve status. **Military personnel** are released from active duty or returned to reserve status. The number of **civilian employees** may be reduced. **Materiel and equipment** may be returned to bases of origin or other reserve/guard units, moth-balled, stored, distributed to other nations through foreign military sales or other security assistance programs, destroyed, sold for scrap, or turned over to the DLA Disposition Services. As with mobilization, assets in the other resource areas are required to support the demobilization of manpower and equipment; but as these support requirements decline, **demobilization activities are accomplished in the other resource areas.** Representative actions in other resource areas are listed in Figure VI-2.

REPRESENTATIVE DEMOBILIZATION ACTIONS IN RESOURCE AREAS	
RESOURCE AREA	**ACTION**
Material/Equipment	War reserve stocks are restored to acceptable levels and redeployed equipment returned to the continental United States (CONUS) is recovered.
Manpower	Cargo handling and port security Reserve Component (RC) are mobilized to support the redeployment of materiel and equipment returned to CONUS. Move returning activated units and personnel to homestations/demobilization sites and return them to reserve duty as appropriate.
Transportation	Strategic air mobility and sealift assets are deactivated or returned to the RC or to the private sector.
Facilities	Buildings are closed, sold, or returned to the private sector or host nations. Staffing is reduced. Contracts for services and utilities are reduced or terminated.
Industrial Base	Contracts are reduced in scope or terminated. Production capacity is laid away or converted to commercial use.
Training Base	Capacity is reduced by closing training centers or reducing staffs and other resources to provide capacity based on future demands.
Health Services	Hospital resources and staffs provided by the National Disaster Medical System or the Department of Veteran Affairs-Department of Defense Contingency Plan are released when no longer required. Medical force structure is deactivated or returned to a reserve status. Contracts with nongovernment and host-nation providers are terminated. Appropriate medical screening and assessment of long-term medical needs for affected personnel is undertaken.
Communications Support	National and joint assets are redeployed. Leased capacity and equipment from commercial sources are reduced in scope or terminated.
Host-Nation Support	Agreements and contracts with host governments or commercial providers are renegotiated or terminated. For specific guidance of acquisition and cross-servicing agreements, refer to Department of Defense Directive 2010.9.
Environment	Military Departments and Department of Defense agencies act to meet environmental standards and regulations with cleanup and other appropriate activities.
Legal Authorities	The President informs Congress when legal authorities invoked for the crisis are no longer needed and are revoked or rescinded.
Funding	Funding required for demobilization and recovery activities is provided in accordance with established peacetime procedures.

Figure VI-2. Representative Demobilization Actions in Resource Areas

SECTION C. MOBILIZATION PLANNER DEMOBILIZATION RESPONSIBILITIES

8. Purpose

This section describes the mobilization planner's role in the demobilization process. Only the manpower portion of the demobilization process is discussed. RC units and individuals are released from active duty under the demobilization process. Although not as time-sensitive as mobilization, demobilization is a complex operation that requires detailed planning and execution.

a. **Demobilization planning should occur during an operation** for the following reasons: expiration of authorized service time; changes in the forces required; or political emphasis to demobilize forces. Mobilization and demobilization may occur simultaneously. Consequently, **each Service must ensure that demobilization plans are flexible, consistent, responsive, and sufficiently comprehensive to meet all contingencies.** From a joint military perspective, **demobilization plans should reflect the post-conflict missions of supported CCDRs** and be synchronized with plans for **recovery, reconstitution, and redeployment operations. DOD policies for the release of reservists and RC units ordered to active duty should first reflect military requirements** and then considerations of equity and fairness for military personnel and their families.

b. Poorly planned and executed demobilization operations will have two major impacts: **degradation to supported operations and reduced support for the RC program.** Demobilization needs to be integrated into redeployment. From a joint military perspective, demobilization plans should reflect the post-conflict missions of supported commanders and be synchronized with plans for battlefield recovery and redeployment operations. Figure VI-3 shows the demobilization activities.

c. A summary of these activities and the specific tasks the mobilization planner

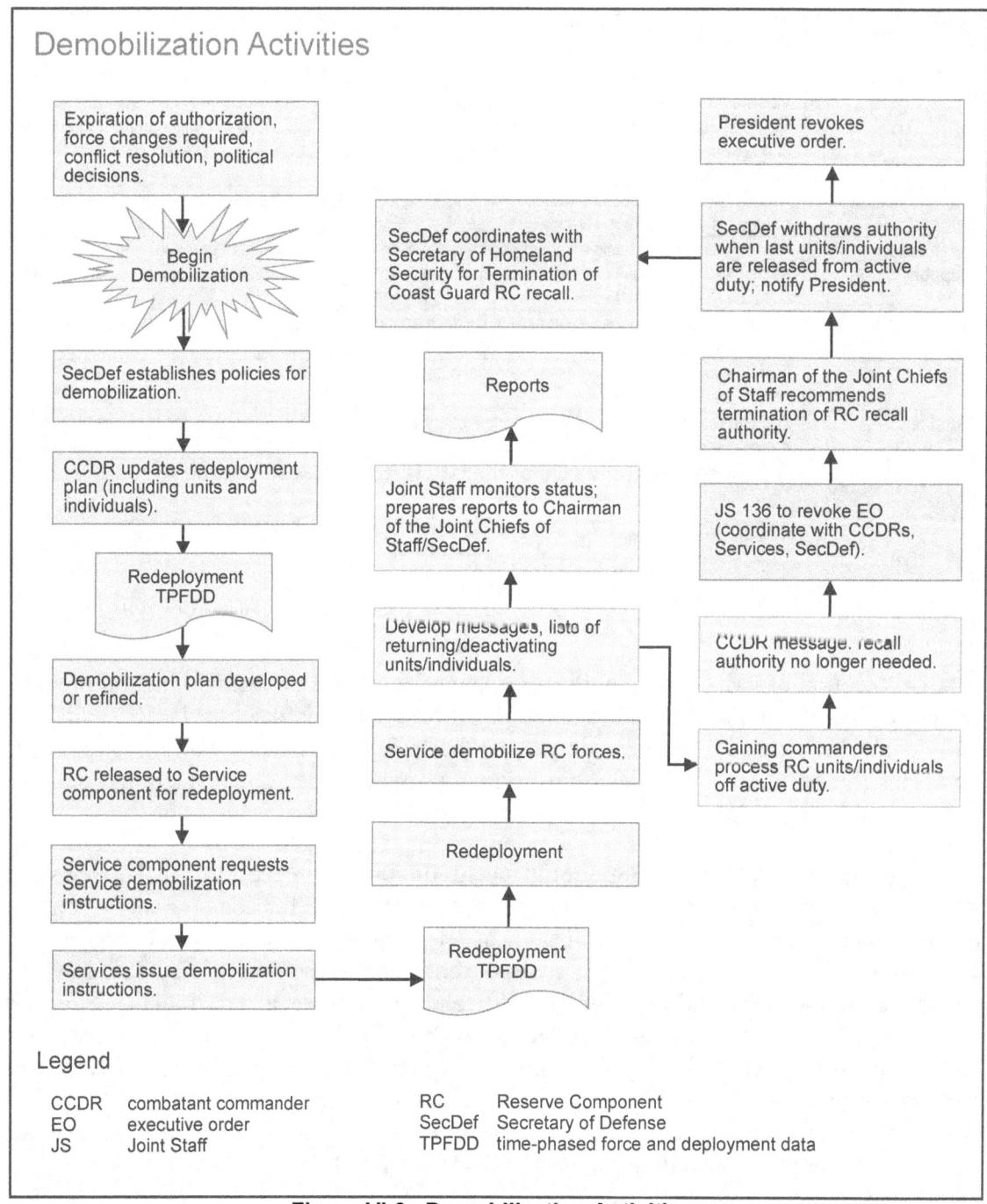

Figure VI-3. Demobilization Activities

accomplishes is found in Annex E, "Demobilization Activities," to Appendix C, "Mobilization Information Management Plan." This summary is a reference of the tasks that must be accomplished at each organizational level to avoid poorly planned and executed demobilization operations.

9. Preliminary Actions

Preliminary actions set the stage for planning and executing a successful demobilization. Primarily, they involve **establishing and disseminating broad guidance** that the mobilization community incorporates into mobilization plans.

a. **Establish Demobilization Concepts and Policies.** Mobilization planners assist in selecting units for demobilization, defining the process, and integrating demobilization into the JOPES (see Figure VI-4). DODD 1235.10, *Activation, Mobilization, and Demobilization of the Ready Reserve,* establishes demobilization policy. This directive states, "Units and individuals of the Ready Reserve ordered to active duty without their consent shall be kept on active duty no longer than absolutely necessary. They shall be released from active duty as promptly as possible, consistent with operational requirements. Individuals activated as a unit should be demobilized as a unit." DODI 1235.12, *Accessing the Reserve Components (RCs),* lists the following demobilization guidelines:

(1) Military Department Secretaries through their Service Chiefs shall ensure that demobilization plans are flexible, consistent, responsive, and comprehensive to meet all challenges.

(2) RC members must meet requirements for separation prior to release from active duty.

(3) Units and individual reservists ordered to active duty should be demobilized at the same mobilization site at which they were initially ordered to report to active duty.

(4) Planners should review DOD policy concerning RC members taking all leave earned during mobilization prior to orders termination unless exceptional circumstances exist. If necessary, orders should be extended to allow accumulated leave to be taken.

Demobilization Policy Issues

- To the extent operationally feasible, redeploy Reserve Component forces first.

- Management of partial units (if only part of unit needed).

- Use of volunteers, contractors, and host-nation support.

- Retaining on active duty only those forces necessary.

Figure VI-4. Demobilization Policy Issues

b. **Provide Input to the JSCP on RC Forces Demobilization.** Mobilization planners address issues such as demobilization support requirements, assumptions on release of forces, RC support of redeployment operations, and times necessary to conduct demobilization. Broad references to demobilization may be appropriate for inclusion in the JSCP while more detailed assumptions and guidance should be included in the classified document, CJCSI 3110.13, *Mobilization Guidance for the Joint Strategic Capabilities Plan (U),* published subsequent to each JSCP.

10. Planning

Demobilization planning involves **reviewing policies** and **establishing procedures** to demobilize. Planners determine operational support requirements and identify the forces to demobilize and those to support the demobilization operations. The planning function is divided into **two subactivities:** plan demobilization force and plan demobilization support (see Figure VI-5.)

a. **Plan Demobilization Force.** This activity establishes the criteria for selecting forces for demobilization, selecting units, and developing a time-phased schedule. This is essentially the same thought process followed during execution. Tasks in planning the demobilization force include:

(1) **Determine Redeployment and Demobilization Strategy.** The Services develop broad concepts for demobilization that are the basis for subsequent detailed planning. These areas include ports, demobilization stations, equipment return policies, medical processing and follow-up, personnel support requirements, and equipment disposition.

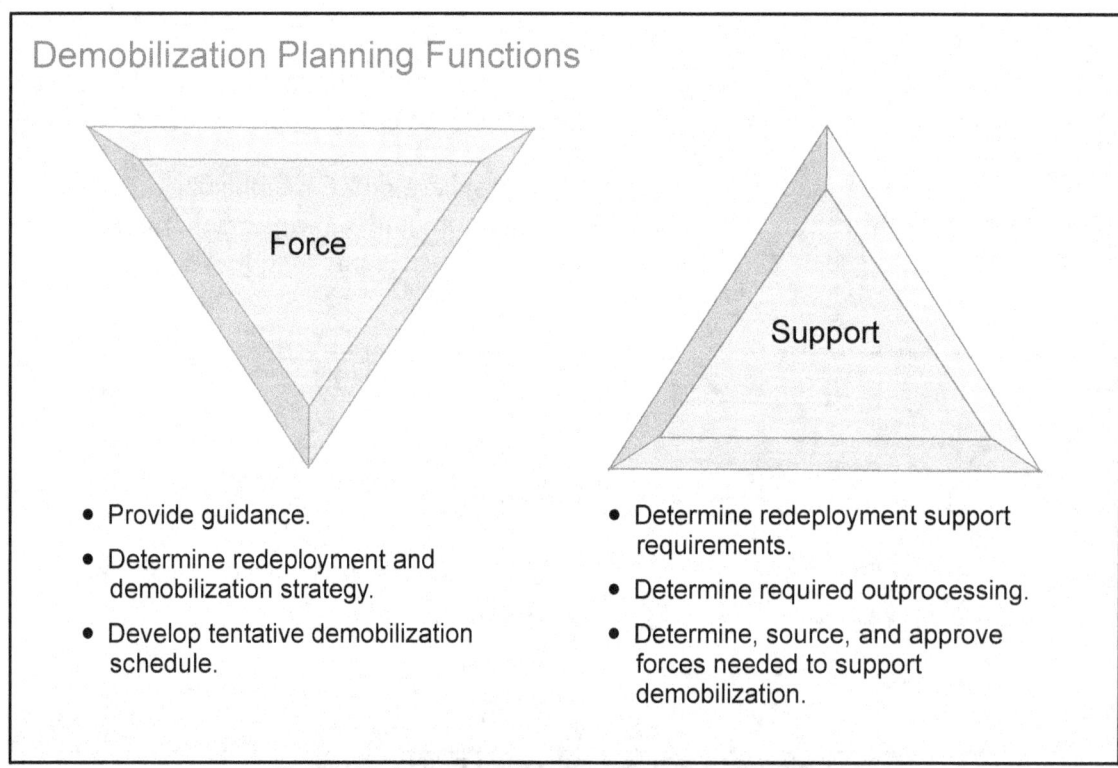

Figure VI-5. Demobilization Planning Functions

For additional guidance on redeployment, see JP 3-35, Deployment and Redeployment Operations.

(a) Mobilization planners must consider carefully those functional areas where most, if not all, of the capability is in the RC. If additional units must be mobilized, shortages of the capability could exist. For example, units may not be available to provide a rotational base in the functional area; in that case, with the onset of another operation, the RC may not be able to support both contingencies.

(b) **Equipment retrograde has manpower implications.** Equipment may be returned from the mission location directly to the unit or may be sent to a processing center for refurbishment. Sometimes equipment may remain in the theater or be transferred to other nations. These considerations may cause personnel from demobilizing units to stay behind to process the equipment. The mobilization planners must incorporate these decisions into demobilization plans.

(2) **Develop Tentative Demobilization Schedule.** The Services create a tentative demobilization schedule based on the assumed level of mobilization. This schedule is used to develop more detailed plans and to estimate resource requirements. Likewise, the commands where the RC forces will be assigned develop schedules to determine support requirements and to ensure the continuation of specific capabilities. Mobilization planners must ascertain if replacement units are required; if they are, the mobilization planners then coordinate with force planners to schedule the overlap with the replacement units.

b. **Plan Demobilization Support.** In this second subactivity mobilization planners consider the specific forces, such as medical, logistic, and transportation, needed to support demobilization; also, they develop more detailed demobilization procedures. During this effort, the mobilization planners must address the support issues such as backfill; ports; demobilization stations; equipment retrograde, processing, and redistribution; outprocessing procedures; and leave policies. **Demobilization support tasks include:**

(1) **Determine Redeployment Support Requirements.** Having determined the RC forces required to support the redeployment of units and individuals, supported CCDRs coordinate with force planners to incorporate these additional requirements into the TPFDD. Other organizations coordinate their requirements with the Services.

(2) **Determine Required Outprocessing.** The Service mobilization planners allot the time and resources necessary for personnel, finance, legal, and medical processing accomplished at the transportation hubs and demobilization stations. They ensure that these factors are integrated into planned movement schedules and that organizations with RC forces are given the information. Service mobilization planners also plan for the homecoming support and ceremonies.

(3) **Determine, Source, and Approve Forces Needed to Support Demobilization.** The Services and CCDRs develop and source the additional manpower needed to support the redeployment, backfill departing units, and support homecoming activities within CONUS.

After the Services approve the additional requirements, these must be integrated with all other mobilization resources to ensure that ceilings are not violated.

11. Execution

a. Before demobilization is executed, mobilization planners must ensure that a unit or individual will not be needed for the operation. Politically, recall of units once demobilized will be difficult to justify; therefore, the Services should be conservative in releasing forces, especially if they involve unique units or skills. In assessing the continuing need for the RC forces, the mobilization planners must consider the entire DOD response, since an RC unit not needed by one component may be useful to another organization.

b. During execution, mobilization planners constantly tailor the demobilization operation envisioned in the plan to the evolving situation. They staff recommendations and obtain decisions regarding units and individuals to be demobilized and adapt the demobilization support structure.

c. Per Figure VI-6, mobilization planners participate in the following execution tasks:

(1) **Educate the Leadership.** Provide the decision makers with information on demobilization plans and policies, including the schedule of units and the number of personnel to be demobilized and those units and personnel already demobilized. When

---

Demobilization Execution

1. Educate the Leadership

   Schedule of units and number of personnel; do not prematurely end emergency and legal basis for mobilization.

2. Review and Modify Demobilization Concepts and Support Plans

3. Monitor Changing Requirements and Theater Backfill Requirements

   Changing operational requirements which affect demobilization, extending on active duty or obtaining rotational replacements.

4. Seek Demobilization Approval

   Combatant commander redeployment plan, Service demobilization list

5. Develop Demobilization Schedule

   Forces, times, release dates, transportation flow

6. Monitor Reserve Component (RC) Mobilizations and Demobilizations

7. Highlight Critical Support Issues in Situation Reports and Other Forums

8. Terminate Legal Authorities

   Upon complete demobilization the Joint Staff will inform Secretary of Defense who may terminate authorization to order RC forces to active duty or inform the President so that Presidential authorization may be withdrawn.

Figure VI-6. Demobilization Execution

---

staffing demobilization recommendations, the mobilization planners ensure that both public and congressional affairs are included in the actions. The mobilization planners should alert their leadership that RC call-ups may continue through all phases of an operation to provide an evolving logistics operations support system which must continue after the combat or crisis phase is complete. It is particularly important to ensure that the leadership does not prematurely recommend ending the emergency which may provide the legal basis for the mobilization of needed RC forces.

(2) **Review and Modify Demobilization Concepts and Support Plans.** The mobilization planners need to update the existing demobilization plan, created in the planning environment, to ensure that the demobilization concepts, policies, and supporting plans are accurate and reflect actual circumstances. They staff the demobilization plans with the appropriate organizations to verify that the users understand the demobilization concept and to enable them to modify their plans and operations.

(3) **Monitor Changing Requirements and Theater Backfill Requirements.** Since demobilization is a fluid process, the mobilization planners continue to review changing operational requirements which may result in units' being demobilized or extended. The supported CCDR must notify the Services, JS, and supporting CCDRs when units or individuals are no longer required or when it is feasible to use alternative manpower sources. If the requirement continues to exist, the appropriate Services, supported CCDR, and supporting CCDRs must request authority to extend the active duty period or obtain rotational units for replacement. DODI 1235.12, *Accessing the Reserve Component,* states that the Military Department Secretaries should ensure that RC forces identified for mobilization are considered for other missions during changes in operational requirements using the following guidelines:

(a) Attempt to redirect the RC unit or member to another requirement 90 days prior to the original mobilization date.

<u>1.</u> Seek to align the RC unit against another like requirement.

<u>2.</u> Consider deploying an RC unit instead of an AC unit.

<u>3.</u> Consider the RC forces for global reallocation if the supported CCDR is unable to reallocate.

(b) De-alert the RC unit as soon as practical if another mission is not available.

(c) Identify and mitigate individual hardships caused by changes to operational requirements.

(4) **Seek Demobilization Approval.** The supported CCDR identifies units and individuals no longer required to support operations in the redeployment plan. Based on the redeployment plan, each Service will develop a demobilization list which is then disseminated within the Service for action. Authority to approve the demobilization list will depend on the Service and the particular operation that may be delegated.

(5) **Develop Demobilization Schedule.** Working closely with the affected organizations and USTRANSCOM, the Services create a demobilization schedule. The schedule includes forces to be demobilized, specific demobilization times, and projected release dates from theater, ports, and demobilization stations. When the schedule is complete, the Services ensure that organizations with RC forces review the schedule and update their supporting plans.

(6) **Monitor RC Mobilizations and Demobilizations.** The mobilization planners start monitoring and reporting on RC units from the beginning of mobilization, and these activities continue through demobilization. This tracking is necessary to obtain information to keep the leadership and Congress apprised of RC actions during the operation. Chapter V, "Mobilization Planning and Execution," Section C, "Mobilization Reporting," covers this function in detail.

(7) **Highlight Critical Support Issues in Situation Reports (SITREPs) and Other Forums.** Using the SITREPs, other JOPES reports, and special functional reports or news groups, the mobilization planner presents conflicts and critical issues to the leadership and the appropriate organization. The mobilization planners' early action enables the responsible individuals and commands to resolve issues expeditiously before they become roadblocks to further activities.

(8) **Terminate Legal Authorities.** Once RC forces are no longer needed to support the operation, demobilization of remaining RC forces will occur. Upon complete demobilization the JS will inform SecDef that there is no longer a need for RC forces in support of the operation. SecDef may terminate the authorization to order RC forces to active duty (if such authorization was granted or delegated to SecDef), direct the Services to terminate the order to activate RC forces, or inform the President so that the Presidential authorization may be withdrawn. This authority automatically is terminated if the President or Congress retracts the original declaration of national emergency. The same legislation that authorizes mobilization implements certain emergency authorities and capabilities. These depend upon the original mobilization authority continuing for their enforcement. Examples of this legislation include those which suspend certain laws pertaining to the promotion, separation, and retirement of active duty personnel (stop loss) and the suspension of Occupational Safety and Health Administration regulations. Until the need for supporting or related authorities is eliminated, planners should urge SecDef, through the CJCS, not to rescind the order or declaration authorizing the call-up.

APPENDIX A
LEGAL AUTHORITIES

1. General

a. Flexible and adaptive mobilization planning requires a range of options available both before and after a national emergency is declared. A broad range of legal authorities support mobilization actions ranging from mobilization for contingency operations, which does not require a declaration of national emergency, as well as full-scale war or other national emergencies. Due to the highly specific nature of legal authorities supporting mobilization actions, it is important that the JPEC and commanders responsible for mobilizing reserve forces consult frequently with staff legal counsel to ensure specific actions are implemented consistent with legal requirements.

b. Mobilization legal authority is available without a declaration of national emergency when invoked by the President or, upon delegation, SecDef, Secretary of a Military Department, or authority designated by the Secretary concerned under the provisions of Title 10, USC, Section 12301. Examples of such authorities are the PRC pursuant to Title 10, USC, Section 12304; the President's option to suspend any provision of law pertaining to promotion, retirement, or separation of a Service member during an RC activation (the stop-loss authority) pursuant to Title 10, Sections 123 and 12305; the Military Department Secretaries' authority to recall regular and reserve military retirees pursuant to Title 10, USC, Sections 12307 and 12308; and authorities requiring priority performance on defense contracts pursuant to Title 50, USC, Chapter 29.

c. A national emergency can be declared by the President, Congress, or both. Current law regarding national emergencies is contained in the National Emergencies Act of 1976 (Title 50, USC, Sections 1601-1651). The act provides that when the President declares a national emergency, the specific authorities must be included in the declaration, or by one or more contemporaneous or subsequent executive orders. Presidential powers are limited to those authorities invoked until the President subsequently announces the invocation of additional specified authorities (Title 50, USC, Section 1631). Congress may terminate the President's declaration at any time with a concurrent resolution and must review the declaration and situation every six months (Title 50, USC, Section 1622).

d. The National Emergencies Act of 1976 greatly reduced the risk that a declaration of national emergency would send overly provocative signals of US intent to adversaries and unduly alarm allies. With the same broad range of emergency powers, the President can now tailor the national response in a crisis, without undue provocation, and convey more accurate signals of US intent to allies as well as adversaries.

e. The War Powers Resolution (WPR) (Title 50, USC, Sections 1541-1548) is a statute, enacted over Presidential veto, that attempts to impose limits upon the President's authority as Commander in Chief over the armed forces to introduce the Armed Forces of the United States into hostilities or potentially hostile situations. Presidents have consistently maintained that the law unconstitutionally intrudes upon Presidential authority. Among other things, the statute attempts to impose consultation and reporting requirements related to the introduction of armed forces into hostilities. While no President has accepted the limitations imposed by the WPR, Presidents have directed DOD to prepare reports "consistent" with the reporting provisions of the WPR. Accordingly, while the statute itself does not control mobilization, the President may require the preparation of a report, "consistent with the provisions of the WPR," regarding the status of US forces, including mobilized RC forces, involved in hostilities.

f. The "Digest of War and Emergency Legislation Affecting the Department of Defense, 2003" lists nearly 400 emergency authorities available for mobilization and crisis planning. This appendix identifies and briefly describes or provides excerpts of many legal authorities relevant to those emergency authorities most likely to affect joint mobilization planning and execution. Additional resources with mobilization authorities include the "Selected Defense-Related Laws" (Volume II—as amended through December 31, 2003), published by the Committee on Armed Services of the US House of Representatives. These references should assist planners, but do not eliminate the need to consult with staff legal counsel.

2. Manpower

Individual and unit members of the RC and retired personnel may be ordered to active duty voluntarily or involuntarily under authorities provided in Title 10, USC. Figure A-1 illustrates RC accessibility.

UNITED STATES CODE—RESERVE COMPONENT ACCESSIBILITY						
Title 10, US Code (USC)	**Armed Forces**					
Statute	**Execution**	**Action**	**Member Consent Required?**	**Passenger Limit?**	**Duration**	**Comment**
Title 10, USC, Section 12301(a) **(Full Mobilization/Ready Reserve)**	In time of war or of national emergency declared by Congress, or when otherwise authorized by law, an authority designated by the Secretary concerned	Order any unit or member not assigned to a unit to active duty	No	No	War, emergency + 6 months	Includes activation of member for training
Title 10, USC, Section 12301(b)	At any time, an authority designated by the Secretary concerned	Order any unit or member not assigned to a unit to active duty	No	No	No more than 15 days/year	
Title 10, USC, Section 12301(d) **(Volunteers/Entire Reserve Force)**	At any time, an authority designated by the Secretary concerned	Order or retain a member on active duty	Yes	No	No limit	Army National Guard and Air National Guard requires consent of governor concerned
Title 10, USC, Section 12302 **(Partial Mobilization/Ready Reserve)**	In time of national emergency declared by the President or when otherwise authorized by law	Order any unit or member not assigned to a unit to active duty	No	Yes. No more than 1,000,000	No more than 24 consecutive months	
Title 10, USC, Section 12304 **(Presidential**	President determines it is necessary to	Order any unit or member not assigned to a unit	No	200,000 overall from	Up to 365 consecutive days	Includes activation of member for

Reserve Call-Up/Selected Reserve)	augment the active forces for any named operational mission or to provide assistance in responding to an emergency involving a terrorist attack or use of weapons of mass destruction (actual or threatened), then he authorizes the Secretary of Defense (SecDef) to call to active duty.	to active duty		Selected Reserve and individual Ready Reserve (IRR) (up to 30, 000 from IRR [must be in special IRR category to be available]).		training. May not be used to provide assistance to United States Government or a State for a serious natural or manmade disaster, accident, or catastrophe unrelated to terrorism.
Title 10, USC, Section 12304a **(Reserve continental United States Emergency Call-Up)**	When a governor requests Federal assistance in responding to a major disaster or emergency, SecDef may order to active duty to respond to the governor's request; no Declaration of National Emergency required	Order any unit or member not assigned to a unit to active duty	No	No	No more than 120 days	Authority to order to Active Duty delegated to the Secretaries of Military Departments. Only applies to the Army Reserve, Navy Reserve, Marine Corps Reserve, and Air Force Reserve
Title 10, USC, Section 12304b **(Preplanned Mobilization Support)**	Secretary of Military Department determines that it is necessary to augment active forces for a preplanned mission in support of a combatant command	Order any unit of the Selected Reserve	No	60,000	No more than 365 consecutive days	Manpower and associated costs of active duty must be included and identified in appropriate fiscal years' defense budget materials
Title 10, USC, Section 12306	In time of emergency when additional capabilities are required as authorized by Section 12301 of this Title, the Secretary concerned with approval of SecDef	Order units and members of the Stand-by Reserve	Yes (but can be superseded by SecDef based on need)	Defined within Title 10, USC, Section 12301	Within parameters of Title 10, USC, Section 12301	Includes activation of member for training

Figure A-1. United States Code—Reserve Component Accessibility

a. **Voluntary Order to Active Duty.** The Military Department Secretaries may order any member of the RC, under their jurisdiction, to active duty with the consent of the member (National Guard [Title 32, USC] also requires consent of the state governor) at any time (Title 10, USC, Section 12301[d]). Funding is the limiting factor for the use of this authority. RC members who are voluntarily on active duty for over three years, or accumulate more than three years over a four-year period, will be counted against AC end strengths. Additionally, RC members desiring to complete additional active duty beyond the three years will require a waiver. RC personnel are exempted from certain officer and enlisted grade limits.

b. **PRC.** The President may activate any unit, and any member not assigned to a unit organized to serve as a unit, of the Selected Reserve or any member of the IRR (designated as essential under regulations prescribed by the Military Department Secretary concerned) without their consent for periods of up to 365 consecutive days when it is determined necessary to augment the active forces for any named operational mission (Title 10, USC, Section 12304). Not more than 200,000 members of the Selected Reserve and the IRR may be on active duty under this section at any one time, of whom not more than 30,000 may be members of the IRR. Specifically, the law provided the authority for the President "to order a unit or member to active duty to provide assistance in responding to an emergency involving a use or threatened use of a weapon of mass destruction; or a terrorist attack or threatened terrorist attack in the US that results, or could result, in significant loss of life or property." The 365 consecutive day limit (increased in Section 522 of the National Defense Authorization Act for Fiscal Year 2007) is tied to each unit or individual and starts with the day that particular unit or individual is called up (therefore rotations are feasible as long as the cap is not exceeded and no personnel are retained involuntarily on active duty in excess of 365 consecutive days). PRC automatically brings the operation within the Title 10, USC definition of a "contingency operation." Presidential declaration of a national emergency is not a prerequisite to authorizing PRC. Recalled reservists under Title 10, USC, Section 12304, authority do not count against end strengths because of the involuntary nature of this recall.

c. **Partial Mobilization Authority.** Following a Presidential declaration of national emergency, the President may order to active duty (other than for training) up to 1,000,000 members of the Ready Reserve, without their consent, for a period not to exceed 24 consecutive months (Title 10, USC, Section 12302). As with PRC, the clock starts for each unit or individual as of the time they enter involuntary active duty.

d. **Reserve CONUS Emergency Call-Up.** When a governor requests Federal assistance in responding to a major disaster or emergency (as those terms are defined in Section 102 of the Robert T. Stafford Disaster Relief and Emergency Assistance Act [42 USC 5122]), SecDef may, without the consent of the member affected, order any unit, and any member not assigned to a unit organized to serve as a unit, of the Army Reserve, Navy Reserve, Marine Corps Reserve, and Air Force Reserve to active duty for a continuous period of not more than 120 days to respond to the Governor's request (Title 10, USC, Section 12304a). The authority to order to active duty per Title 10, USC, Section 12304a has been delegated to the Secretaries of the Military Departments per SecDef Memorandum, Delegation of Authority under Title 10, USC, Section 12304a, dated 7 March 2013.

e. **Preplanned Mobilization Support.** When the Secretary of a Military Department determines that it is necessary to augment the active forces for a preplanned mission in support of a CCMD, the Secretary may order any unit of the Selected Reserve, without the consent of the members, to active duty for not more than 365 consecutive days (Title 10, USC, Section 12304b). The manpower and associated costs of such active duty must be specifically included and identified in the defense budget materials for the fiscal year or years in which such units are anticipated to be ordered to active duty. Not more than 60,000 members of the RCs may be on active duty under this section at one time.

f. **Full Mobilization Authority.** The President, under Title 10, USC, Section 12301, and the additional Title 10, USC, and Title 50, USC, Emergency Authorities, upon a congressional declaration of national emergency or war may authorize the Military Department Secretaries, or their designees, to order to active duty any member of the RC, without their consent, for the duration of the emergency or war plus six months (Title 10, USC, Section 12301[a]). Members in inactive or retired status are not recallable under this provision without the approval of SecDef.

g. **Total Mobilization Authority.** The President, upon a congressional declaration of national emergency or war, and with passage of legislation authorizing force expansion, may authorize the Services to add new forces and personnel necessary to achieve national security objectives.

h **Active Duty Retiree Recall.** Under Title 10, USC, Section 688 and regulations established by SecDef, the Military Department Secretaries are authorized, at any time, to recall (without their consent) retired members of the ACs, members of the Retired Reserve who were retired under Title 10, USC, Sections 1293, 3911, 3914, 6323, 8911, or 8914, or members of the Fleet Reserve and Fleet Marine Reserve (this includes reserve members who retired from active duty with less than 20 years under Temporary Early Retirement Authority). This authorization does not require a declaration of national emergency or war.

i. **Retired Reserve Recall.** Reserve members in a retired status (other than those who fall under the provisions of Active Duty Retiree Recall described above) may be recalled involuntarily to active duty only in time of war or national emergency as declared by Congress. This authority requires that the Military Department Secretaries, with the approval of SecDef, first determine that there are not enough qualified reservists available, in the required categories, to fill the required billets (Title 10, USC, Section 12301).

j. **Recall of the Standby Reserve.** Units and members in the Standby Reserve may be ordered to active duty (other than for training) only as provided in Title 10, USC, Sections 12301(a) and 12306. In addition, this authority requires that the Military Department Secretaries first determine that there are not enough qualified members in the Ready Reserve in the required categories who are readily available.

k. **Call to Active Duty of Delayed Entry Program Personnel.** Qualified personnel with no prior military service may be enlisted as untrained members of the IRR for up to 365 days before reporting for active duty under Title 10, USC, Section 513. All such persons may be ordered to active duty under all provisions of the law and regulations applying to the IRR.

l. **Stop-Loss Authority.** This authority stops normal attrition of experienced military personnel through expiration of enlistments, retirements, and other routine releases from active duty. With this authority, during any period RC members have been involuntarily ordered to active duty, the President may suspend any provision of law relating to retirement, promotion, separation of military personnel determined to be essential to the national security (Title 10, USC, Section 12305).

m. **Conscription.** If Congress deems it necessary under the Selective Service Act (Title 50, USC, Sections 451-473), the SSS can begin involuntarily drafting eligible, nonexempt men for military service. Repeal of Title 50, USC, Section 467(c) is necessary before the SSS may initiate an involuntary draft of NPS personnel.

n. **Uniformed Services Employment and Reemployment Rights Act (USERRA).** USERRA (Title 38, USC, Sections 4301-4335) is a federal law intended to ensure that persons who serve or have served in the Armed Forces (AC or RC) or other "uniformed services" are:

(1) Not disadvantaged in their civilian careers because of their service.

(2) Promptly reemployed in their civilian jobs upon their return from duty.

(3) Not discriminated against in employment based on past, present, or future military service.

o. **The Service member's Civil Relief Act** provides a number of statutory protections for activated military members, especially for members of the National Guard and reserve forces. Examples include a 6 percent rate cap on obligations, a 90 day stay of proceedings, and the right to terminate auto and residential leases under certain circumstances. Members should contact their servicing staff judge advocate for further information.

3. The Defense Production Act of 1950

Authority for expanding capability or capacity in the materiel and equipment, transportation, and industrial base resource areas is provided by the Defense Production Act. This act (Title 50 Appendix, USC, Sections 2061-2171), which has been periodically revised and renewed by Congress, provides the basis for the DPAS. It authorizes the President, in peace, conflict, and war, to divert national resources deemed critical to the national defense from civil to military use, and reorder economic priorities to provide for the national defense and national security. Specifically, the President may require private sector providers of materials and services, identified as essential and critical to national defense, to give priority performance to defense contracts and orders. The President may also authorize USG departments, like DOD, DOT, and Department of Commerce, to guarantee loans needed by defense contractors to expedite production, deliveries, or service.

4. Facilities

There are three fundamental emergency authorities available to facilitate construction projects required to expand facilities during mobilization.

a. **Emergency Construction Authority.** The Secretary of a Military Department is authorized by Title 10, USC, Section 2803 to execute emergency military construction projects if the Secretary determines: the project is vital to the national security or to the protection of health, safety, or the quality of the environment; and the requirement for the project is so urgent that to defer it for the next military construction authorization act would be inconsistent with national security or to the protection of health, safety, or the quality of the environment. Per Title 10, USC, Section 2803 the maximum amount a Secretary may obligate in any fiscal year is $50 million, taken from the unobligated balances of funds appropriated for military construction.

b. **Contingency Construction.** SecDef is authorized by Title 10, USC, Section 2804 to execute contingency military construction projects, before a declaration of national emergency, upon determination that the deferral of the projects would be inconsistent with national security or national interest. Specific funding limits can change each year. Members should consult with staff judge advocate to determine current contingency construction limits and requirements.

c. **Construction Authority in the Event of a Declaration of War or National Emergency.** In the event of a declaration of war or the declaration by the President of a national emergency requiring use of the Armed Forces, SecDef may undertake construction projects needed to support the Armed Forces without specific legislative authorization. Such projects, however, must be able to be completed within the total amount of unobligated military construction funds, including funds appropriated for family housing per Title 10, USC, Section 2808.

d. **Reacquisition and Condemnation of Real Property.** There are more than 60 permanent laws in the USC authorizing the President, SecDef, or specified Secretary of a Military Department to reacquire specific parcels of former federal property for defense purposes. In general, the availability of these authorities is contingent on a declaration of national emergency by the President or Congress or the existence of a state of war. As a practical matter, many of these sites have been rendered virtually unusable for defense purposes, because of commercial development undertaken over the years since some of these laws were enacted (some as early as 1925). The US Army Corps of Engineers, however, maintains a list of properties still usable for national defense purposes. In addition, Title 10, USC, Section 2663 authorizes Secretaries of the Military Departments to bring condemnation proceedings, in courts with appropriate jurisdiction, to acquire land or facilities deemed necessary for a variety of defense purposes including construction of training sites, and production of explosives or other munitions of war.

5. **Training Base Expansion**

There are no legal authorities specifically directed to expansion of the military training base in connection with mobilization. Training base expansion activities, however, may require activation of RC training units and individual manpower, expansion of facilities, equipment, and transportation resources, under emergency authorities pertaining to these resource areas. Training base expansion plans must also take into account the provision of Title 10, USC, Section 671, which requires a minimum of 12 weeks of basic training (or its equivalent), with some exceptions, before assigning any member of the Armed Forces to duties OCONUS. The intent of this law is to ensure that no Service member is assigned overseas without basic combat skills.

6. Health Services

a. Activation of RC health services, medical units, and individuals is governed by the same authorities for mobilizing other manpower skills as discussed in paragraph 2, "Manpower."

b. The President is authorized by Title 42, USC, Section 217 to declare the commissioned corps of the USPHS a military service in time of war or national emergency.

c. Under the provisions of the DVA and DOD Health Resources Sharing and Emergency Operations Act (Title 38, USC, Section 8110[a]), the DVA will make beds available to DOD for the care of military casualties.

d. The NDMS, established and administered by the Department of Health and Human Services under the authority of Executive Order 12656, *Assignment of Emergency Preparedness Responsibilities,* provides backup support to DOD and DVA in caring for military casualties. Although not legally obligated, nonfederal public and private hospitals have agreed to provide about 100,000 beds to augment DOD and DVA resources, if needed in an emergency. This commitment is triggered when SecDef determines military casualties threaten to overburden the DOD and DVA systems.

7. Communications

The Communications Act of 1934 (Title 47, USC, Section 606) authorizes the President, during times of emergency or war, to exercise extraordinary management or control over national telecommunications resources to meet requirements for telecommunications services beyond those normally provided by individual commercial suppliers or government agencies.

8. Host-Nation Support

Authorities for obtaining HNS manpower and services are provided for in various treaties and other international agreements to which the US is a signatory, including numerous logistic agreements.

Refer to JP 4-08, Logistics in Support of Multinational Operations, *for further HNS information.*

9. Environment

Major environmental protection statutes affecting mobilization are discussed in Chapter IV, "Resource Areas." While the President has the authority, when in the national interest, to authorize an exemption from certain environmental laws, seeking such an exemption would require highest-level action within DOD. Executive Order 12088, *Federal Compliance with Pollution Control Standard*s (as amended by Executive Order 13148,

Greening the Government Through Leadership in Environmental Management), and DOD policy require full compliance with applicable environmental laws and regulations, unless an authorized exemption or exception is obtained.

10. Funding

The following emergency authorities are available to DOD to provide essential funding for mobilization and other emergency defense expenditures.

a. **Budget Supplemental.** SecDef may submit additional appropriations requests to Congress to meet urgent requirements.

b. **Budget Amendment.** SecDef may submit budget revisions to Congress before the congressional appropriations process has been completed.

c. **Reprogramming.** SecDef may reprogram funds within appropriations thresholds established by Congress to meet the requirements of any emergency. Reprogramming actions above established thresholds must be submitted to Congress for approval.

d. **Transfer Authority.** Authority and thresholds for transferring funds between appropriations are established in the current appropriations act. Transfers that exceed thresholds require congressional approval.

e. **Deficiency Authority (Feed and Forage Act).** Title 41, USC, Section 11, permits DOD to obligate funds in excess of amounts authorized and appropriated to cover necessities of the current year, under circumstances in which appropriations for clothing, subsistence, fuel, quarters, transportation, or medical and hospital supplies are exhausted. This authority ensures the availability of sufficient funds to care for the unexpected increases in DOD personnel strength as a result of a crisis and mobilization.

Intentionally Blank

APPENDIX B
AUTOMATED TOOLS

1. General

The JPEC:

a. Prepares systems to monitor forces and phases of the crisis or mobilization.

b. Plans for information management systems to consolidate IT support for all functional areas of a mobilization, thereby reducing the total number of varying systems carrying similar data.

c. Reduces administrative functions to meet mobilization surge requirements.

d. Reviews IT procedures that stimulate development of effective communications system capabilities for enhanced crisis response.

e. Designs and tests mobilization-related IT systems to ensure their ability to operate effectively.

2. Planning

The Services mobilize, train, equip, and prepare forces, including the RC, for movements in CONUS to meet scheduled deployment and employment dates. Movement of mobilized RC units from home station to mobilization station may be a support installation responsibility. The Military Surface Deployment and Distribution Command, a USTRANSCOM component command, is responsible for planning intra-CONUS movements to support mobilization and deployment using OPLAN TPFDD files and intra-CONUS movement data. The Services and DOD agencies will provide significant RC mobilization-related movement requirements to USTRANSCOM. The supported CCDR prioritizes and validates requirements to USTRANSCOM. USTRANSCOM then coordinates with the support installation and supported CCDR to resolve movement constraints and advises CJCS of transportation capabilities in CONUS. During deployment, USTRANSCOM monitors the movement of forces and materiel by common-user lift from home station to the destination. In this circumstance, USTRANSCOM will immediately be able to identify a conflict so resolution can be obtained from CJCS and the appropriate CCDR.

3. Reporting Systems Supporting Mobilization

a. **JOPES Database.** As part of APEX, the JOPES deployment database contains the necessary information on forces, materiel, and filler and replacement personnel movement requirements to support execution. The database reflects information contained in the refined TPFDD from deliberate planning or developed during the various phases of CAP, and the movement schedules or tables developed by the transportation component commands to support the deployment of required forces, personnel, and materiel.

b. **Joint Industrial Mobilization Planning Process (JIMPP).** JIMPP is the generic term for the planning and analytic process to be used by the Services, DOD agencies, and JS to:

(1) Prepare industrial mobilization plans linked to deliberate planning and CAP procedures, development, and execution.

(2) Provide the analytical framework to perform the industrial analyses required by the Joint Strategic Planning System and OSD.

(3) Establish baseline national industrial base capability assessments tied to potential military demand.

(4) JIMPP is used during planning to conduct capability and risk assessments, emergency procurement budget mechanisms, time-phased requirements lists, and narrative COAs. Output may be forwarded to OSD and other USG departments or agencies for use in broader industrial mobilization planning. As an analytical tool, JIMPP allows planners to address "what if" questions from both the supply and demand sides. Expected outputs of the process include supply-side option summaries for level of mobilization, estimates of a mobilizable force, and assessments of plan feasibility. JIMPP consists of three components: a requirements module, which produces weapons and munitions requirements, associated shortfalls, replacement of losses, and consumption rates; a vendor-level module for specific options and capabilities (compares each item requirement with its production rate and produces surge and mobilization requirements and shortfalls); and an industry-level module for a macroeconomic sector-level analysis of mobilization requirements and capabilities for 240 industrial sectors.

c. **Joint Engineering Planning and Execution System (JEPES).** JEPES is the developmental engineer component of the Global Combat Support System—Joint. As the Global Combat Support System–Joint is refined, engineer planners at the CCMDs and their components will utilize the Joint Construction Management System (JCMS) to plan for the required engineering force, construction material, and facilities to support OPLANs. Further, JCMS can be used to:

(1) Assess time-phased facility requirements based on an OPLAN.

(2) Analyze and assess engineering support by comparing facility requirements to in-theater facility assets and host nation, contract, and troop engineering capability.

d. **Joint Flow and Analysis System for Transportation (JFAST).** JFAST provides rapid analysis of the transportation feasibility of OPLANs and COAs before validation by the supported CCMD and transportation acceptance by USTRANSCOM.

e. **Department of Defense Emergency Authorities Retrieval and Analysis System (DEARAS).** DEARAS is operated by the Air Force as Executive Agent for DOD. This system is a compilation of publicly available DOD, joint, and Service publications. The DEARAS database is unclassified and can be downloaded and installed on a portable stand-alone computer. This legal research resource is intended for a legal professional working in a deployed or contingency environment where Internet connectivity is very limited or nonexistent.

f. **Global Status of Resources and Training System (GSORTS).** GSORTS is an information management system designed to support the decision-making process of the President, SecDef, and CJCS. GSORTS supports the registration of units, reporting of basic unit identity elements, monitoring of unit status, and distribution of unit information throughout the JPEC. Distributed information includes unit location, strength, readiness factor, and category levels for equipment and personnel. Individual units update the GSORTS database by a Defense Information Systems Network communications link. The system constitutes the single automated tool for maintaining and updating unit status.

g. **Global Decision Support System (GDSS).** GDSS is the worldwide command and control system for the execution of strategic airlift and air refueling during peacetime, contingencies, and war. GDSS is used to monitor and manage all operational DOD air mobility missions throughout the world including all organic, commercial, and air refueling missions.

See JP 3-35, Deployment and Redeployment Operations, *for more information on enabler tools.*

h. **Defense Readiness Reporting System (DRRS).** DRRS is a mission-focused, capabilities-based Internet application that provides the CCDRs, Services, Joint Chiefs of Staff, and other key DOD users a collaborative environment in which to evaluate the readiness and capability of the Armed Forces to carry out assigned tasks. This enables users to find units which are both ready and available for deployment in support of a given mission.

i. **Enhanced Status of Resources and Training System (ESORTS).** ESORTS feeds DRRS and provides a more complete readiness assessment system by directly measuring outputs—the ability to conduct a task or mission to the prescribed standard—along with inputs. The system is designed to come much closer to the goal of understanding "ready for what?" ESORTS provides a vehicle for each organization from individual units to combined forces to report on its ability to achieve the performance standard of its mission-essential tasks under the conditions of the assignments.

Intentionally Blank

APPENDIX C
MOBILIZATION INFORMATION MANAGEMENT PLAN

1. General

a. When circumstances dictate the formation of an MWG, a MIMP will be developed. The MIMP is designed to provide guidance on information systems used in mobilization planning and execution. It identifies the flow of information related to mobilization during a crisis action.

b. Misconceptions regarding the mobilization process and the resultant procedures are as prevalent as are the abundant sources of information. This plan identifies the various sources and uses of existing mobilization data to enhance awareness and understanding of this data.

c. The MIMP is published separately by the JS J-4.

2. Information Holders

Each Service has visibility over its personnel as the entry-point for mobilization processing. Additionally, numerous DOD components track mobilization activities data, such as the following:

a. JS J-4. As the proponent for mobilization activities of the JS, manages mobilization ceilings associated with partial mobilization and PRCs and requisite reporting to Congress.

b. Assistants to CJCS for National Guard Matters and Reserve Matters. Established as part of the National Defense Authorization Act of Fiscal Year 1998, these two assistants advise the CJCS on National Guard and reserve matters, respectively.

c. JS J-35 [Deputy Directorate for Regional, Force Management, and Future Operations]. The JS office of primary responsibility for all readiness reporting applications and systems.

d. JS J-7 [Operational Plans and Joint Force Development Directorate]. JS Directorate for Joint Force Development, office of primary responsibility for the Joint Lessons Learned Program, and program manager for JLLIS, the joint lessons learned system of record.

e. CJCS Legal Counsel. Maintains visibility over proper application of statutory requirements as they pertain to mobilization.

f. CJCS Legislative Assistant. Maintains visibility over mobilization activities to support congressional inquiries.

g. CJCS Public Affairs. Maintains visibility over mobilization activities to support media inquiries.

h. OSD (Reserve Affairs). OSD (Reserve Affairs) receives personnel status reports from the Services. This report provides daily visibility of the number and category of RC personnel called up under Title 10, USC, authority.

i. DFAS. Maintains visibility of all Service members for pay purposes.

j. Defense Manpower Data Center. Maintains visibility of all Service members for congressional and other special interest reporting purposes.

3. Information Flow

a. The flow of mobilization information depends on the operational environment—crisis or noncrisis.

b. When in a crisis environment such as a wartime or other scenario, information related to mobilization activities typically flows through the current operations team/current action team.

c. During a noncrisis scenario, information related to mobilization activities typically flows through legislative affairs or public affairs channels and then to the Service manpower and reserve affairs departments for resolution. Public affairs issues will be presented at the DOD level.

4. Information Tools

A wide array of recurring products are created by the information holders, containing data specific to mobilization. The MIMP identifies the specific MOBREPs generated by the various information holders to expand awareness of these products in managing mobilization activities. Information holders are encouraged to inform the JS J-4 of any changes regarding recurring products related to mobilization activities to allow the MIMP to remain current.

Intentionally Blank

ANNEX A TO APPENDIX C
PLANNING ACTIVITIES

Mobilization Planning Community	Develop Concept	Develop Plan	Develop Supporting Plan	Analyses
PLANNING ACTIVITIES				
Common Activities (For all)	• Provide pre-planning input • Provide combatant commander strategic concept feedback • Plan participation			• Determine levels of mobilization necessary to support projected RC force requirements • Answer questions on the justification of RC call-ups • Validate or refute defense planning guidance and/or Joint Strategic Capabilities Plan planning assumptions
Joint Staff	• Confirm tasking for RC requirements summary			• Review completed operation plan and most probable FDO
Service		• Source specific RC units	• Requirements for complete operation plan and most probable FDO: • RC in area of responsibility • RC unit personnel in TPFDD • RC non-unit personnel in supplemental TPFDD • Move the force, assist mobilization, deployment, and/or sustainment • Backfill	
Supported Command	• Draft, coordinate, and issue the supplemental TPFDD letter of instruction		• Comply with requirements for operation plan • FDO determination	
Subordinate and/or Supporting Commands US Transportation Command Components Joint Task Force			• Requirements for complete operation plan and most probable FDO: • Move the force • Assist mobilization, deployment, and/or sustainment • Backfill	

Legend

FDO   flexible deterrent option
RC   Reserve Component
TPFDD time-phased force and deployment data

Figure C-A-1. Planning Activities

Intentionally Blank

ANNEX B TO APPENDIX C
RESERVE COMPONENT CALL-UP DECISION-MAKING ACTIVITIES

RESERVE COMPONENT CALL-UP DECISION-MAKING ACTIVITIES							
Mobilization Planning Community	Pre-Mobilization Review and Coordination	Educate Senior Leadership on RC Potential	Interpret Policies for Use of RCs	Confirm Pre-Planned Mobilization Capabilities	Recommend Changes in Peacetime Budgeting Priorities	Modify Demobilization Policy to Suit Contingency	Prepare Decision Packages
Common Activities (For all)	• Identify point of contact network • Convene preliminary meetings focused on "what if" questions using current information • Analyze lessons learned from similar crises • Consider potential supporting requirements • Manage media relations and coordinate with public affairs officer	• Conduct meetings and/or briefings on RC mobilization policies: availability, mobilization and deployment criteria, and the different categories of RC and their potential use	• Review and modify call-up instructions and procedures • Recommend modifications and exceptions to policy • Coordinate with legal counsel • Review judge advocate general policies and/or procedures for "conscientious objectors" and Soldiers and Sailors Act	• Estimate ability of mobilization activities to meet plan schedule • Identify capability shortfalls	• Review unfunded mobilization requirements • Coordinate with resource area proponents for adjustments to internal funding priorities	• Initiate planning for the return of RC to civilian status	• Respond to information requests as appropriate
Joint Staff	• Become familiar with RC call-up procedures • Be prepared to recommend level of call-up	• Review legal authorities in Title 10, US Code • Review mobilization plans, policies, and procedures • Brief leadership on call-up authorities and specific qualities of RCs	• Identify opportunities for joint use of Service mobilization assets • Monitor the development of RC deployment criteria	• Confirm monitoring and reporting systems: coordinate reporting requirements	• Seek opportunities for cross-Service utilization of RC assets	• Seek opportunities for cross-Service utilization of RC demobilization facilities and assets	• Prepare draft decision package • Staff draft decision package with Services • Forward package to Chairman of the Joint Chiefs of Staff
Service	• Review monitoring and reporting requirements • Consider sources of immediate manpower augmentation	• Review Service mobilization doctrine for unit and individual call-up • Review civilian mobilization	• Develop deployment criteria consistent with the needs of the CCDR • Review Service Readiness	• Validate projected RC requirements of OPLAN within DOD guidance	• Coordinate with program assessment and budget office to raise visibility of unfunded mobilization requirements	• Determine redeployment criteria for RC unit equipment and personnel • Coordinate with National Committee for Employer	• Coordinate on Draft Decision Package

		plans	Processing policies • Validate policies for use of civilians, contractors, and other non-DOD agencies		•Recommend changes to eliminate shortages	Support of the Guard and Reserve	
	• Start planning for demobilization						
Supported Command	• Ensure RC OPLAN support requirements are projected	• Ensure theater-unique requirements are known to force providers	• Review mobilization doctrine and policy • Brief command on RC capabilities and limitations to support plan	• Validate projected RC requirements of OPLAN	• Support efforts to adjust funding priorities	• Develop redeployment priorities and schedule	• Coordinate on Draft Decision Package
Subordinate and/or Supporting Commands US Transportation Command Components Joint Task Force	• Review RC requirements projected by CCDR	• Review RC requirements to move force, backfill displaced units, and assist in the mobilization and deployment process • Brief leadership on RC mobilization doctrine	• Review mobilization doctrine and policy • Brief command on RC capabilities and limitations to support plan	• Validate projected RC requirements	• Support efforts to adjust funding priorities	• Review demobilization doctrine • Support redeployment and/or demobilization operations	• Coordinate on Draft Decision Package • Begin to evaluate need for subsequent RC augmentation

Legend

CCDR   combatant commander
DOD   Department of Defense
OPLAN   operation plan
RC   Reserve Component

Figure C-B-1. Reserve Component Call-Up Decision-Making Activities

ANNEX C TO APPENDIX C
MOBILIZATION ACTIVITIES

MOBILIZATION ACTIVITIES	
Mobilization Planning Community	**Execution**
Common Activities (For all)	• Coordinate with public affairs officer • Monitor unit and individual mobilization schedules • Review missions needed to be supported to ensure all requirements have been met
Joint Staff	• Monitor force requirements • Coordinate and refine execution policies and guidance
Service	• Coordinate and refine execution policies and guidance • Monitor and adjust call-up procedures for individuals • Manage call-up against ceilings • Ensure that TPFDD is updated as combatant commander requirements change • Notify congressional delegations for call-up prior to public affairs announcement
Supported Command	• Ensure theater-unique requirements that impact upon the RC are known to force providers • Ensure that TPFDD is updated as requirements change
Subordinate and/or Supporting Commands US Transportation Command Components Joint Task Force	• Ensure that TPFDD is updated as requirements change • Ensure unique requirements that impact upon the RC are known to force protection
Legend RC Reserve Component TPFDD time-phased force and deployment data	

Figure C-C-1. Mobilization Activities

Internationally Blank

ANNEX D TO APPENDIX C
MONITORING AND REPORTING ACTIVITIES

MONITORING AND REPORTING ACTIVITIES		
Mobilization Planning Community	**Monitoring**	**Reporting**
Common Activities (For all)	• Monitor the status of mobilization • Monitor unit and individual demobilization schedules	• Gather information to respond to various requests • Report Reserve Component (RC) forces no longer needed
Joint Staff	• Monitor force requirements • Determine any special information requirements and assign reporting requirements	• Direct Services provide input for Report to Congress (partial mobilization) • Prepare Report to Congress • Provide mobilization information as required • Review military manpower mobilization and accession status report
Service	• Monitor force requirements • Monitor sourcing	• Enter data into RC Apportionment tables • Submit mobilization report to Chairman of the Joint Chiefs of Staff • Report on problems in providing forces • Submit input data to Chairman of the Joint Chiefs of Staff for Presidential Report to Congress
Supported Commands	N/A	• Enter data into RC Apportionment tables
Subordinate and/or Supporting Commands US Transportation Command Components Joint Task Force	N/A	N/A

Figure C-D-1. Monitoring and Reporting Activities

Intentionally Blank

ANNEX E TO APPENDIX C
DEMOBILIZATION ACTIVITIES

DEMOBILIZATION ACTIVITIES			
Mobilization Planning Community	**Preliminary Actions**	**Planning**	**Execution**
Common Activities (For all)	• Establish demobilization concepts and policies	• Provide guidance	• Educate the leadership • Review and modify demobilization concepts and support plans
Joint Staff	• Provide input to the Joint Strategic Capabilities Plan		• Monitor Reserve Component (RC) mobilizations and demobilizations • Validate support and rotational requirements • Resolve any conflicts in resource alignment • Propose that the Secretary of Defense rescind legal authorities
Service		• Determine redeployment and demobilization strategy • Develop demobilization schedule	• Determine required out processing • Determine, source, and approve forces to support demobilizations	• Monitor RC mobilizations and demobilizations • Monitor changing requirements and theater backfill requirements • Execute demobilization schedule • Estimate and source support and rotational requirements • Seek demobilization approval • Solve or adjudicate conflicting resource claims
Supported Command		• Develop tentative demobilization schedule	• Determine redeployment support requirements • Determine, source, and approve forces to support demobilizations	• Offer candidates for demobilization • Estimate and source support and rotational requirements • Highlight critical support issues in situation reports
Subordinate and/or Supporting Commands US Transportation Command Components Joint Task Force		• Develop tentative demobilization schedule	• Determine redeployment support requirements • Determine, source, and approve forces to support demobilizations	• Offer candidates for demobilization • Estimate and source support and rotational requirements • Highlight critical support issues in situation reports

Figure C-E-1. Demobilization Activities

Intentionally Blank

APPENDIX D
MOBILIZATION WORKING GROUP

1. Purpose

a. When circumstances dictate, the CJCS will establish an ad hoc MWG. The MWG is designed to enhance communications between OSD, the JS, CCDRs, and Services when military operations warrant the use of involuntarily recalled RC forces and/or the federalization of National Guard units.

b. The MWG will be chaired by the JS J-4 and will convene to address mobilization issues resulting from military operations.

c. Members are encouraged to raise issues in the forum of the MWG as appropriate to enhance a DOD-wide approach regarding the mobilization of RC forces and/or the federalization of National Guard units.

2. Participants

a. The MWG will be chaired by the JS J-4.

b. The following offices/components are requested to provide at least one representative to the MWG:

(1) JS J-1 [Manpower and Personnel Directorate], JS J-3, JS J-4, assistants to CJCS for National Guard and reserve matters, JS Legal Counsel, and JS Public Affairs.

(2) OSD (Reserve Affairs).

(3) CCDR liaison officers, as required.

(4) Services—Army, Navy, Marine Corps, Air Force, and Coast Guard (when considered for Title 10, USC, mobilization as a service in the Department of the Navy), as required.

(5) National Guard Bureau representatives.

(6) USPHS representatives.

Intentionally Blank

APPENDIX E
MOBILIZATION ESTIMATE

SECURITY CLASSIFICATION
Originating Organization

Place of Issue

Date-Time Group, Month, Year
Mobilization Estimate Number _____

References:

    a. Maps and Charts.

    b. Other Pertinent Documents.

1. ( ) Mission. State the CCDR's missions, taken from the mission analysis, planning guidance, or other statements. (Look specifically for RC and federalized National Guard unit missions.)

2. ( ) Situations and Considerations

    a. ( ) Assumptions

    b. ( ) Mobilization Situation

        (1) ( ) Availability of Manpower.

        (2) ( ) Transportation.

        (3) ( ) Equipment/Materiel.

        (4) ( ) Health Services.

        (5) ( ) Facilities.

        (6) ( ) Industrial Base.

        (7) ( ) Training Base.

        (8) ( ) Communications.

        (9) ( ) HNS.

        (10) ( ) Environment.

        (11) ( ) Legal Authorities.

(12) ( ) Funding.

(13) ( ) Security Issues.

3. ( ) Mobilization Analysis of COAs. Make an orderly examination of the manpower, equipment/materiel, transportation, health services, industrial, training bases, communications, and legal authority resource areas that affect the proposed COAs to determine the manner and degree of that effect. The objective of this analysis is to determine whether the mobilization requirements can be met and to isolate the implications that should be considered by the CCDR in the commander's estimate.

a. ( ) Analyze each COA from a mobilization point of view.

b. ( ) The mobilization factors in subparagraph 2b are the factors to be analyzed for each COA under consideration. Examine these factors realistically from the standpoint of time-phased requirements versus actual or programmed capabilities that may affect the mobilization COA.

c. ( ) Throughout the analysis, keep mobilization considerations foremost in mind. The analysis is not intended to produce a decision. It is intended to ensure that all applicable mobilization factors have been properly considered and to serve as the basis for comparisons in paragraph 4.

4. ( ) Comparison of COAs

a. ( ) List the impact that manpower mobilization for each level, including PRC, has on the other resource areas from a logistic directorate's point of view.

b. ( ) Develop a work sheet that identifies decisions that must be made in all resource areas based on the mobilization decision.

5. ( ) Conclusions

a. ( ) State whether the mission set forth in paragraph 1 can be supported from a mobilization standpoint.

b. ( ) State which mobilization COA can best be supported from a transportation, equipment/materiel, and health services standpoint.

c. ( ) Identify the major resource area deficiencies that must be brought to the attention of the CCDR. Provide recommendations from the Services as to the methods to eliminate or reduce the impact of those deficiencies.

(Signed) _____

APPENDIX F
REFERENCES

The development of JP 4-05 is based upon the following primary references:

1. General

a. The Constitution of the United States of America.

b. Title 10, USC.

c. Title 14, USC.

d. Title 32, USC.

e. Title 37, USC.

f. Title 42, USC.

g. Title 46, USC, Chapter 27.

h. Title 47, USC, Section 606.

i. Title 50, USC.

2. Department of Defense Publications

a. DPG.

b. GEF.

c. GFMIG.

d. DODD 1200.17, *Managing the Reserve Components as an Operational Force.*

e. DODD 1235.10, *Activation, Mobilization, and Demobilization of the Ready Reserve.*

f. DODD 1235.13, *Management of the Individual Ready Reserve (IRR) and the Inactive National Guard (ING).*

g. DODD 1250.01, *National Committee for Employer Support of the Guard and Reserve (NCESGR).*

h. DODD 1332.35, *Transition Assistance for Military Personnel.*

i. DODD 4500.54E, *DOD Foreign Clearance Program (FCP).* (https://www.fcg.pentagon.mil/fcg.cfm).

j. DODI 1100.22, *Policy and Procedures for Determining Workforce Mix.*

k. DODI 1215.06, *Uniform Reserve, Training, and Retirement Categories.*

l. DODI 1225.06, *Equipping the Reserve Forces.*

m. DODI 1235.09, *Management of the Standby Reserve.*

n. DODI 1235.11, *Management of Individual Mobilization Augmentees (IMAs).*

o. DODI 1235.12, *Accessing the Reserve Component (RC).*

p. DODI 4715.6, *Environmental Compliance.*

q. DODI 5158.05, *Joint Deployment Process Owner.*

r. DODI 8260.03, *Organizational and Force Structure Construct (OFSC) for Global Force Management (GFM).*

s. DOD 4500.54-G, *Department of Defense Foreign Clearance Guide.*

3. **Chairman of the Joint Chiefs of Staff Publications**

a. CJCSI 1301.01E, *Joint Individual Augmentation Procedures.*

b. CJCSI 3100.01B, *Joint Strategic Planning System.*

c. CJCSI 3110.13D, *Mobilization Guidance for the Joint Strategic Capabilities Plan.*

d. CJCSM 3122.01A, *Joint Operation Planning and Execution System (JOPES), Volume I (Planning Policies and Procedures).*

e. CJCSM 3122.02D, *Joint Operation Planning and Execution System (JOPES), Volume III (Time-Phased Force and Deployment Data Development and Deployment Execution).*

f. CJCSM 3130.03, *Adaptive Planning and Execution (APEX) Planning Formats and Guidance.*

g. CJCSM 3150.13C, *Joint Reporting Structure—Personnel Manual.*

h. CJCS 3150.25, *Joint Lessons Learned Program.*

i. JP 1, *Doctrine for the Armed Forces of the United States.*

j. JP 1-0, *Joint Personnel Support.*

k. JP 1-06, *Financial Management Support in Joint Operations.*

l. JP 3-0, *Joint Operations.*

m. JP 3-34, *Joint Engineer Operations*.

n. JP 3-35, *Deployment and Redeployment Operations*.

o. JP 4-0, *Joint Logistics*.

p. JP 4-02, *Health Services*.

q. JP 4-08, *Logistics in Support of Multinational Operations*.

r. JP 4-10, *Operational Contract Support*.

s. JP 5-0, *Joint Operation Planning*.

4. Service Publications

a. Army Mobilization and Operations Planning and Execution System.

b. Chief of Naval Operations Instruction S3061.1E, *Navy Capabilities and Mobilization Plan (NCMP) (U)*.

c. Marine Corps Mobilization, Activation, Integration, and Deactivation Plan.

d. Air Force War and Mobilization Plan.

e. Commandant, USCG Instruction, M3061.1, *Coast Guard Manpower Mobilization and Support Plan*.

Intentionally Blank

APPENDIX G
ADMINISTRATIVE INSTRUCTIONS

1. User Comments

Users in the field are highly encouraged to submit comments on this publication to: Joint Staff J-7, Deputy Director, Joint Education and Doctrine, ATTN: Joint Doctrine Analysis Division, 116 Lake View Parkway, Suffolk, VA 23435-2697. These comments should address content (accuracy, usefulness, consistency, and organization), writing, and appearance.

2. Authorship

The lead agent and Joint Staff doctrine sponsor for this publication is the Director for Logistics J-4.

3. Supersession

This publication supersedes JP 4-05, *Joint Mobilization Planning*, 22 March 2010.

4. Change Recommendations

a. Recommendations for urgent changes to this publication should be submitted:

   TO: JOINT STAFF WASHINGTON DC//J7-JED//

b. Routine changes should be submitted electronically to the Deputy Director, Joint Education and Doctrine, ATTN: Joint Doctrine Analysis Division, 116 Lake View Parkway, Suffolk, VA 23435-2697, and info the lead agent and the Director for Joint Force Development, J-7/JED.

c. When a Joint Staff directorate submits a proposal to the CJCS that would change source document information reflected in this publication, that directorate will include a proposed change to this publication as an enclosure to its proposal. The Services and other organizations are requested to notify the Joint Staff J-7 when changes to source documents reflected in this publication are initiated.

5. Distribution of Publications

Local reproduction is authorized, and access to unclassified publications is unrestricted. However, access to and reproduction authorization for classified JPs must be IAW DOD Manual 5200.01, Volume 1, *DOD Information Security Program: Overview, Classification, and Declassification,* and DOD Manual 5200.01, Volume 3, *DOD Information Security Program: Protection of Classified Information.*

6. Distribution of Electronic Publications

a. Joint Staff J-7 will not print copies of JPs for distribution. Electronic versions are available on JDEIS Joint Electronic Library Plus (JEL+) at https://jdeis.js.mil/jdeis/index.jsp (NIPRNET) and http://jdeis.js.smil.mil/jdeis/index.jsp (SIPRNET), and on the JEL at http://www.dtic.mil/doctrine (NIPRNET).

b. Only approved JPs are releasable outside the combatant commands, Services, and Joint Staff. Release of any classified JP to foreign governments or foreign nationals must be requested through the local embassy (Defense Attaché Office) to DIA, Defense Foreign Liaison.

c. JEL CD-ROM. Upon request of a joint doctrine development community member, the Joint Staff J-7 will produce and deliver one CD-ROM with current JPs. This JEL CD-ROM will be updated not less than semi-annually and when received can be locally reproduced for use within the combatant commands, Services, and combat support agencies.

GLOSSARY
PART I—ABBREVIATIONS AND ACRONYMS

AC	Active Component
ACSA	acquisition and cross-servicing agreement
AE	aeromedical evacuation
AOR	area of responsibility
APEX	Adaptive Planning and Execution
CAP	crisis action planning
CCDR	combatant commander
CCMD	combatant command
CEW	civilian expeditionary workforce
CIL	critical item list
CJCS	Chairman of the Joint Chiefs of Staff
CJCSI	Chairman of the Joint Chiefs of Staff instruction
CJCSM	Chairman of the Joint Chiefs of Staff manual
COA	course of action
CONUS	continental United States
CSA	combat support agency
CSS	combat service support
DCMA	Defense Contract Management Agency
DEARAS	Department of Defense Emergency Authorities Retrieval and Analysis System
DFAS	Defense Finance and Accounting Service
DISA	Defense Information Systems Agency
DLA	Defense Logistics Agency
DOD	Department of Defense
DODD	Department of Defense directive
DODI	Department of Defense instruction
DOT	Department of Transportation
DPAS	Defense Priorities and Allocation System
DPG	Defense Planning Guidance
DPO	distribution process owner
DRRS	Defense Readiness Reporting System
DVA	Department of Veterans Affairs
ESORTS	Enhanced Status of Resources and Training System
FDO	flexible deterrent option
GCC	geographic combatant commander
GDSS	Global Decision Support System
GEF	Guidance for Employment of the Force

GEOINT	geospatial intelligence
GFM	global force management
GFMIG	Global Force Management Implementation Guidance
GI&S	geospatial information and services
GSORTS	Global Status of Resources and Training System
HNS	host-nation support
IA	individual augmentee
IMA	individual mobilization augmentee
IRR	Individual Ready Reserve
ISA	individual Service augmentee
IT	information technology
JCMS	Joint Construction Management System
JDPO	joint deployment process owner
JEPES	Joint Engineer Planning and Execution System
JFAST	Joint Flow and Analysis System for Transportation
JFC	joint force commander
JIA	joint individual augmentee
JIMPP	joint industrial mobilization planning process
JLLIS	Joint Lessons Learned Information System
JMPAB	Joint Materiel Priorities and Allocation Board
JOPES	Joint Operation Planning and Execution System
JOPP	joint operation planning process
JP	joint publication
JPEC	joint planning and execution community
JS	Joint Staff
JSCP	Joint Strategic Capabilities Plan
LOI	letter of instruction
MARAD RRF	Maritime Administration Ready Reserve Force
MIMP	Mobilization Information Management Plan
MMG	Department of Defense Master Mobilization Guide
MOBREP	mobilization report
MWG	mobilization working group
NATO	North Atlantic Treaty Organization
NCESGR	National Committee of Employer Support for the Guard and Reserve
NCS	National Communications System
NDMS	National Disaster Medical System (DHHS)
NDS	national defense strategy
NGA	National Geospatial-Intelligence Agency
NMS	national military strategy

NPS	nonprior service
NSS	national security strategy
OASD(RA)	Office of the Assistant Secretary of Defense (Reserve Affairs)
OCONUS	outside the continental United States
OPLAN	operation plan
OPORD	operation order
OSD	Office of the Secretary of Defense
PPBE	Planning, Programming, Budgeting, and Execution
PRC	Presidential Reserve Call-up
RC	Reserve Component
SecDef	Secretary of Defense
SECHS	Secretary of Homeland Security
SITREP	situation report
SOF	special operations forces
SSS	Selective Service System
TPFDD	time-phased force and deployment data
TRO	training and readiness oversight
UCP	Unified Command Plan
UN	United Nations
USC	United States Code
USCG	United States Coast Guard
USERRA	Uniformed Services Employment and Reemployment Rights Act
USG	United States Government
USPHS	United States Public Health Service
USSOCOM	United States Special Operations Command
USTRANSCOM	United States Transportation Command
WPR	War Powers Resolution

PART II—TERMS AND DEFINITIONS

activation. Order to active duty (other than for training) in the federal service. (JP 1-02. SOURCE: JP 4-05).

active duty. Full-time duty in the active military service of the United States, including active duty or full-time training duty in the Reserve Component. Also called **AD.** (Approved for incorporation into JP 1-02.)

active duty for training. A tour of active duty that is used for training members of the Reserve Component to provide trained units and qualified persons to fill the needs of the Armed Forces in time of war or national emergency and such other times as the national security requires. Also called **ADT.** (Approved for incorporation into JP 1-02.)

active status. None. (Approved for removal from JP 1-02.)

annual screening. None. (Approved for removal from JP 1-02.)

annual training. None. (Approved for removal from JP 1-02.)

backfill. Reserve Component units and individuals recalled to replace deploying active units and/or individuals in the continental United States and outside the continental United States. (JP 1-02. SOURCE: JP 4-05)

consumption rate. The average quantity of an item consumed or expended during a given time interval, expressed in quantities by the most appropriate unit of measurement per applicable stated basis. (JP 1-02. SOURCE: JP 4-05)

critical item list. A prioritized list identifying supply items and weapon systems that assist Service and Defense Logistics Agency selection of supply items and systems for production surge planning, or in operational situations, used by the combatant commander and/or subordinate joint force commander to cross-level critical supply items between Service components. Also called **CIL.** (Approved for incorporation into JP 1-02.)

delayed entry program. A program under which an individual may enlist in a Reserve Component of a military service and specify a future reporting date for entry on active duty that would coincide with availability of training spaces and with personal plans such as high school graduation. Also called **DEP.** (JP 1-02. SOURCE: JP 4-05)

demobilization. 1. The process of transitioning a conflict or wartime military establishment and defense-based civilian economy to a peacetime configuration while maintaining national security and economic vitality. 2. The process necessary to release from active duty, or federal service, units and Reserve Component members who were ordered to active duty, or called to federal service. (Approved for incorporation into JP 1-02.)

federal service. A term applied to National Guard members and units when called to active duty to serve the United States Government under Article I, Section 8 and Article II,

Section 2 of the Constitution and Title 10, United States Code, Sections 12401 to 12408. (JP 1-02. SOURCE JP 4-05)

full mobilization. Expansion of the active Armed Forces resulting from action by Congress and the President to mobilize for the duration of the emergency plus six months all Reserve Component units and individuals in the existing approved force structure, as well as all retired military personnel, and the resources needed for their support to meet the requirements of a war or other national emergency involving an external threat to the national security. (Approved for incorporation into JP 1-02.)

home station. The permanent location of active duty units and Reserve Component units. (Approved for incorporation into JP 1-02.)

Inactive National Guard. None. (Approved for removal from JP 1-02.)

inactive status. Status of reserve members on an inactive status list of a Reserve Component or assigned to the Inactive Army National Guard. (Approved for incorporation into JP 1-02.)

individual mobilization augmentee. An individual reservist attending drills who receives training and is preassigned to an Active Component organization, a Selective Service System, or a Federal Emergency Management Agency billet that must be filled on, or shortly after, mobilization. Also called **IMA.** (Approved for incorporation into JP 1-02.)

Individual Ready Reserve. A manpower pool consisting of individuals who have had some training or who have served previously in the Active Component or in the Selective Reserve, and may have some period of their military service obligation remaining. Also called **IRR.** (Approved for incorporation into JP 1-02.)

industrial mobilization. The transformation of industry from its peacetime activity to the industrial program necessary to support the national military objectives. (Approved for incorporation into JP 1-02.)

industrial preparedness. The state of preparedness of industry to produce essential materiel to support the national military objectives. (JP 1-02. SOURCE: JP 4-05)

industrial preparedness program. Plans, actions, or measures for the transformation of the industrial base, both government-owned and civilian-owned, from its peacetime activity to the emergency program necessary to support the national military objectives. Also called **IPP.** (Approved for incorporation into JP 1-02.)

joint individual augmentee. An unfunded temporary duty position (or member filling an unfunded temporary duty position) identified on a joint manning document by a supported combatant commander to augment headquarters operations during contingencies. Also called **JIA.** (Approved for inclusion in JP 1-02.)

mobilization. 1. The process of assembling and organizing national resources to support national objectives in time of war or other emergencies. 2. The process by which the

Armed Forces of the United States or part of them are brought to a state of readiness for war or other national emergency, which includes activating all or part of the Reserve Component as well as assembling and organizing personnel, supplies, and materiel. Also called **MOB.** (Approved for incorporation into JP 1-02.)

mobilization base. The total of all resources available, or that can be made available, to meet foreseeable wartime needs. (Approved for incorporation into JP 1-02.)

mobilization exercise. None. (Approved for removal from JP 1-02.)

mobilization site. The designated location where a Reserve Component unit or individual mobilizes or moves after mobilization for further processing, training, and employment. (Approved for incorporation into JP 1-02.)

mobilization staff officer. None. (Approved for removal from JP 1-02.)

mobilization station. The designated military installation to which a Reserve Component unit or individual is moved for further processing, organizing, equipping, training, and employment and from which the unit or individual may move to an aerial port of embarkation or seaport of embarkation. (JP 1-02. SOURCE: JP 4-05)

partial mobilization. Expansion of the active Armed Forces resulting from action by Congress (up to full mobilization) or by the President (not more than 1,000,000 for not more than 24 consecutive months) to mobilize Ready Reserve Component units, individual reservists, and the resources needed for their support to meet the requirements of a war or other national emergency involving an external threat to the national security. (Approved for incorporation into JP 1-02.)

Presidential Call-up. None. (Approved for removal from JP 1-02.)

Presidential Reserve Call-up. Provision of a public law (Title 10, United States Code, Section 12304) that provides the President a means to activate, without a declaration of national emergency, not more than 200,000 members of the Selected Reserve and the Individual Ready Reserve (of whom not more than 30,000 may be members of the Individual Ready Reserve), for not more than 365 days to meet the requirements of any operational mission, other than for disaster relief or to suppress insurrection. Also called **PRC.** (Approved for incorporation into JP 1-02.)

production base. The total national industrial production capacity available for the manufacture of items to meet materiel requirements. (JP 1-02. SOURCE: JP 4-05)

Ready Reserve. The Selected Reserve and Individual Ready Reserve liable for active duty as prescribed by law (Title 10, United States Code, Sections 10142, 12301, and 12302). (Approved for incorporation into JP 1-02.)

remain-behind equipment. Unit equipment left by deploying forces at their bases when they deploy. (JP 1-02. SOURCE: JP 4-05)

reserve. 1. Portion of a body of troops that is kept to the rear, or withheld from action at the beginning of an engagement, in order to be available for a decisive movement. 2. Members of the uniformed Services who are not in active service but who are subject to call to active duty. 3. Portion of an appropriation or contract authorization held or set aside for future operations or contingencies and, in respect to which, administrative authorization to incur commitments or obligations has been withheld. (Approved for incorporation into JP 1-02.)

Reserve Component. The Armed Forces of the United States Reserve Component consists of the Army National Guard of the United States, the Army Reserve, the Navy Reserve, the Marine Corps Reserve, the Air National Guard of the United States, the Air Force Reserve, and the Coast Guard Reserve. Also called **RC.** (Approved for incorporation into JP 1-02.)

Reserve Component category. None. (Approved for removal from JP 1-02.)

Retired Reserve. All reserve members who receive retirement pay on the basis of their active duty and/or reserve service; those members who are otherwise eligible for retirement pay but have not reached age 60 and who have not elected discharge and are not voluntary members of the Ready Reserve or Standby Reserve. (Approved for incorporation into JP 1-02.)

Selected Reserve. Those units and individuals within the Ready Reserve designated by their respective Services and approved by the Joint Chiefs of Staff as so essential to initial wartime missions that they have priority over all other reserves. (Approved for incorporation into JP 1-02.)

selective mobilization. Expansion of the active Armed Forces resulting from action by Congress or the President to mobilize Reserve Component units, Individual Ready Reservists, and the resources needed for their support to meet the requirements of a domestic emergency that is not the result of an enemy attack. (Approved for incorporation into JP 1-02.)

Standby Reserve. Those units and members of the Reserve Component (other than those in the Ready Reserve or Retired Reserve) who are liable for active duty only, as provided in Title 10, United States Code, Sections 10151, 12301, and 12306. (JP 1-02. SOURCE: JP 4-05)

stop-loss. Presidential authority under Title 10, United States Code, Section 12305, to suspend laws relating to promotion, retirement, or separation of any member of the Armed Forces determined essential to the national security of the United States, to include reservists if serving on active duty under Title 10, United States Code authorities for Presidential Reserve Call-up, partial mobilization, or full mobilization. (Approved for incorporation into JP 1-02.)

time-phased force and deployment list. Appendix 1 to Annex A of the operation plan, which identifies types and/or actual units required to support the operation plan and indicates origin and ports of debarkation or ocean area. Also called **TPFDL.** (Approved for incorporation into JP 1-02.)

total mobilization. Expansion of the active Armed Forces resulting from action by Congress and the President to organize and/or generate additional units or personnel beyond the existing force structure, and the resources needed for their support, to meet the total requirements of a war or other national emergency involving an external threat to the national security. (Approved for incorporation into JP 1-02.)

training unit. None. (Approved for removal from JP 1-02.)

JOINT DOCTRINE PUBLICATIONS HIERARCHY

JP 1
JOINT DOCTRINE
JP 1-0
PERSONNEL
JP 2-0
INTELLIGENCE
JP 3-0
OPERATIONS
JP 4-0
LOGISTICS
JP 5-0
PLANS
JP 6-0
COMMUNICATIONS SYSTEM

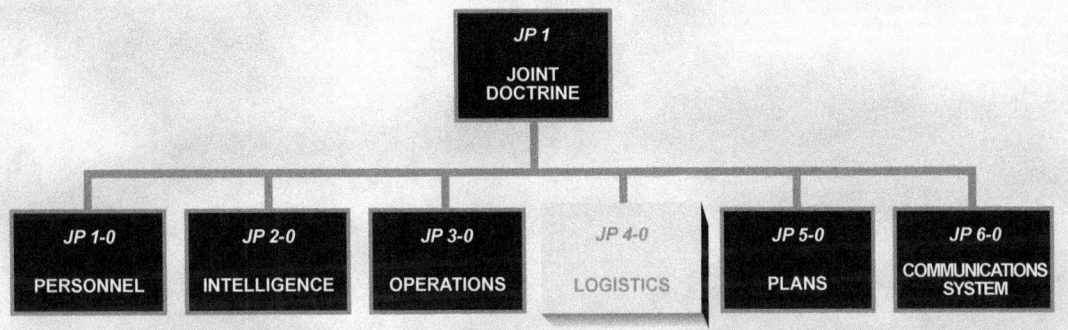

All joint publications are organized into a comprehensive hierarchy as shown in the chart above. **Joint Publication (JP) 4-05** is in the **Logistics** series of joint doctrine publications. The diagram below illustrates an overview of the development process:

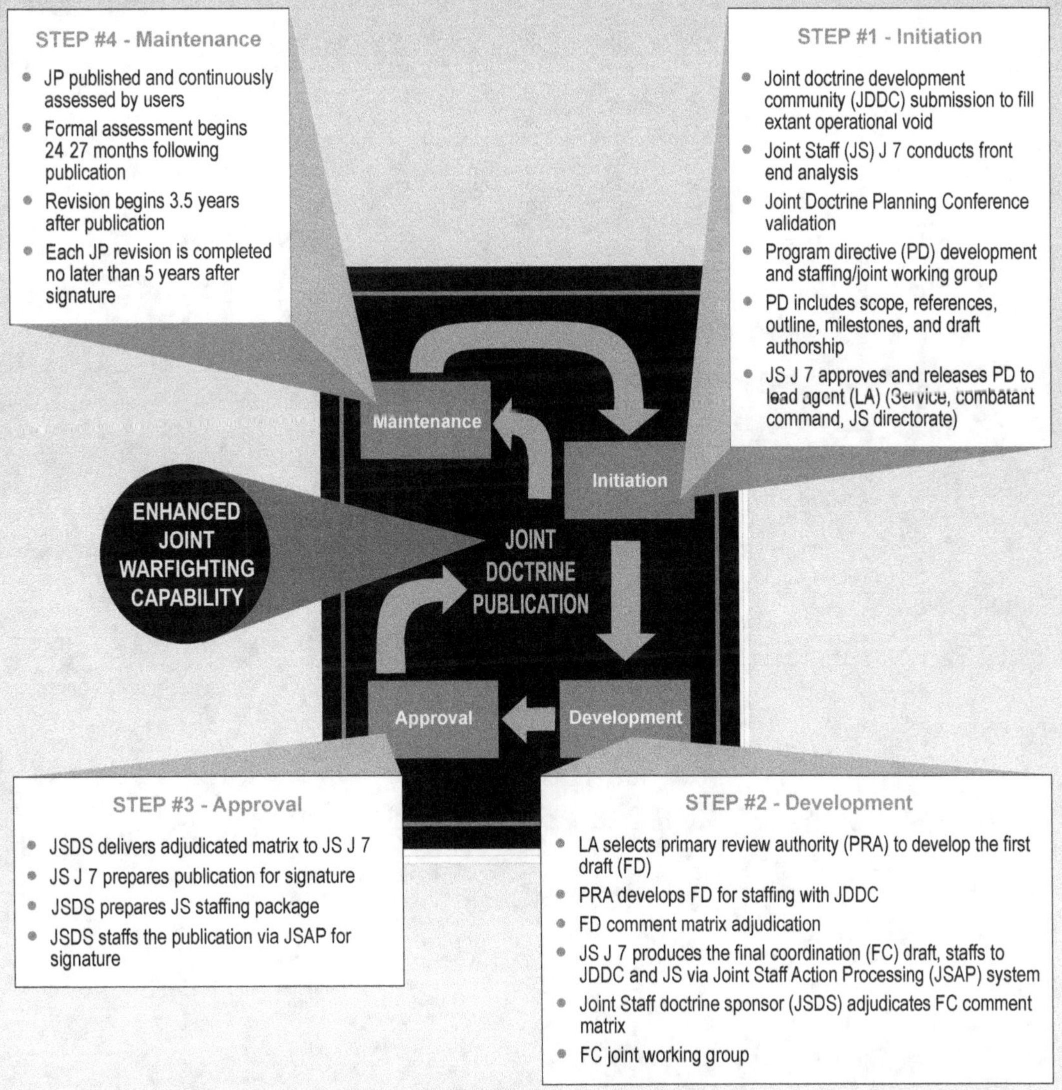

STEP #4 - Maintenance
JP published and continuously assessed by users
Formal assessment begins 24 27 months following publication
Revision begins 3.5 years after publication
Each JP revision is completed no later than 5 years after signature
STEP #1 - Initiation
Joint doctrine development community (JDDC) submission to fill extant operational void
Joint Staff (JS) J 7 conducts front end analysis
Joint Doctrine Planning Conference validation
Program directive (PD) development and staffing/joint working group
PD includes scope, references, outline, milestones, and draft authorship
JS J 7 approves and releases PD to lead agent (LA) (Service, combatant command, JS directorate)
Maintenance
Initiation
ENHANCED JOINT WARFIGHTING CAPABILITY
JOINT DOCTRINE PUBLICATION
Approval
Development
STEP #3 - Approval
JSDS delivers adjudicated matrix to JS J 7
JS J 7 prepares publication for signature
JSDS prepares JS staffing package
JSDS staffs the publication via JSAP for signature
STEP #2 - Development
LA selects primary review authority (PRA) to develop the first draft (FD)
PRA develops FD for staffing with JDDC
FD comment matrix adjudication
JS J 7 produces the final coordination (FC) draft, staffs to JDDC and JS via Joint Staff Action Processing (JSAP) system
Joint Staff doctrine sponsor (JSDS) adjudicates FC comment matrix
FC joint working group